Sunset
Add·a·Room Book

Successful Ideas for More Living Space

By the Editors of Sunset Books
and Sunset Magazine

Lane Publishing Co., Menlo Park, California

If you're thinking of adding on . . .

When you need more living space, adding to your present home can be the best possible answer. It's not the only answer, of course—you could move to a bigger house, or you could build one. But with real estate costs soaring and a diminishing amount of land available, staying put and adding on is the choice of more and more homeowners, and it may be right for you.

Naturally, along with the price of everything else, costs of construction and materials are rising—the bill for your completed addition is going to be significantly higher today than it would have been just a couple of years ago. But, as a general rule, the sledge hammer of inflation won't strike you as hard for an add-on project as it will if you buy or build a new house. And new rooms will add not only space but cash value to your home.

So if you're thinking of adding on, this is the book for you. Its pages are crammed with practical advice to help you see an add-on project through from beginning to end. Do you want to cut costs without cutting quality? See the special feature on money-saving tips. Do you want to make energy conservation a part of your plan? See the feature on letting the sun work for you.

You'll enjoy browsing the gallery of additions, the selected projects that are successful both esthetically and functionally. Beyond that, they represent a wide range of possibilities, so you're likely to find more than one that will approximate your circumstances and inspire you.

Many people helped in the preparation of this book. Central among them are the homeowners and architects whose projects fill its pages. Special thanks go to architect Roger East, Arnold Anderson, Terry Millar, Rick Morrall, Donald Johnson, and Julie Anne Gold.

Supervising Editor: Jack McDowell
Research and Text: Buff Bradley

Design: Steve Reinisch
Illustrations: Clyde Foles, Stephanie Reed
Photography: Jack McDowell
(pages 24–25 by Rob Super)

Cover: Bay window expansion adds more room, brings in more light. Architect: George Cody. Photograph: Darrow M. Watt

Editor, Sunset Books: David E. Clark

Second Printing September 1979

Contents

SECTION I

Planning Your Home Improvement

Adding a room to your house can be a challenging and rewarding project. Whether you do all the work yourself or team up with professionals, you're bound to feel a certain excitement as you see your house taking on a new shape and a new ambience — a shape and ambience more suited to your needs and life style.

But adding on is no tea party. Few people have the inclination, or the opportunity, simply to turn over their home to an architect or building designer, announce what they want done, and leave for a few weeks in the Caribbean, then to return to a newly completed addition. For months you may be meeting with architects, enduring the presence of contractors' crews in and around your house, and fussing with an endless list of details.

No book can promise to simplify all the details or eliminate all the problems that are bound to arise during the process of adding to your house. The aim of this one is to help minimize the hassles. Section I details the basic considerations in planning and managing a room addition project. Section II surveys a number of additions already built.

The first section will tell you how to evaluate your present space situation, how to choose an architect or designer, how to learn about building codes and zoning restrictions, how to hire a contractor, and much more.

In the second section you'll find case histories of more than 40 homes that have been expanded by room additions. This idea section is intended to stimulate your thinking and planning. It's unlikely that any of the houses will be exactly like yours, but within the broad range of homes presented, you're likely to find some that approximate your situation.

Included in both sections are special features that focus on a number of interesting and important considerations, from energy conservation to ways of saving money.

Three basic types of room additions are covered: rooms added on new foundations at ground-floor level; second-story additions; and new rooms created from existing attics and basements.

How to get started

You might have any number of reasons for wanting to add space to your house. In the late 19th century, Mrs. Sarah Winchester (of the riflemaker's family) became convinced that she would not die as long as she continued to build onto her house. She started with eight rooms and finished with 160, $5½ million later. Your reasons are likely to be more conventional than Mrs. Winchester's (who did, by the way, die).

You may need more space because your family has grown. You may need an office so you can work at home. You may want a special kind of room — a game room, a studio, or a music room. You might want to take better advantage of a view or of the sunlight. And, for one reason or another, you've decided that you don't want to buy a new home to get the additional room.

After determining that they need more space, some families have gone hunting for houses that satisfy their needs more suitably than their present ones and have found nothing they like. Only then have they decided that adding on is the best solution. Others may be reluctant to leave behind their present neighborhoods, friends, schools, or recreational facilities just to get into a bigger house. Still others just can't afford to build or buy a new home, and are forced by circumstance to stay put.

What's involved in adding on?

To give you a general idea of what's involved in adding on, we've outlined the major tasks that need to be done — each point on the list is discussed in detail later on. The three outlines describe three different situations. One enumerates what you'll need to do if you design and build the addition yourself; another lists your tasks if you'll be working with an architect who will design the addition and oversee construction; the third tells what you'll need to do if you work with a contractor who will turn your ideas into a design and then do the building.

Of course, each of these three situations contains countless variables. For instance, you might have an architect draw up the plans and then supervise the construction yourself; or you might do your own plans, have them drafted professionally, and then turn the construction over to a contractor. The outlines here are intended as general descriptions rather than exhaustively detailed ones; your particular circumstances will determine what tasks you do, in which order, and how the work is divided among you and the various people who work for you on the project.

Doing it all yourself. Though the following list is not all inclusive, it will serve as a guide to the formidable array of tasks you'll face if you're going to do your own addition from start to finish.

• Determine all the purposes you want the new room(s) to serve.
• Study your house and property, making interior and exterior scale drawings.
• Check your property title for deed restrictions and easements.
• Make preliminary sketches of the new addition.
• Take sketches to the local building department to learn if the proposed addition violates the building code or zoning restrictions.
• Prepare final plans of the proposed addition.
• Get necessary permits from the building inspector's office.
• List all the materials you'll need, then go to suppliers and price them.
• Arrange for financing the addition.
• Arrange for workers' compensation insurance and withholding tax if necessary.
• Purchase materials and begin construction.
• Arrange for the building inspector to check various stages of work at appropriate times.

If you hire an architect or building designer to design the structure and monitor construction, you shorten the list considerably; of course, you also increase the cost of the project.

Using an architect or building designer. Three of the jobs listed below are optional. Some homeowners prefer to let the architect do them; others do them personally so they can work in a more informed way with the architect or designer.

• Determine all the purposes you want the new room(s) to serve (optional).
• Study your house and property, making interior and exterior scale drawings (optional).
• Check your property title for deed restrictions and easements.
• Make preliminary sketches of the new addition (optional).
• Choose an architect.
• After you and your architect agree on final plans, he or she will arrange for bids on the project, advise you on the hiring of a contractor, and monitor the project through to completion.
• Arrange for financing.

Working with a contractor. The third alternative, one many homeowners use, involves your working with a contractor to design an addition, and also your doing some of the labor. The contractor's design won't be nearly as expensive as an architect's, and if you intend your addition to be simple and straightforward you may see little reason to engage an architect or building designer. Doing some of the labor yourself will also save you money.

• Determine all the purposes you want the new room(s) to serve (optional).
• Study your house and property, making interior and exterior scale drawings (optional).
• Check your property title for deed restrictions and easements.
• Make preliminary sketches of the new addition (optional).
• Choose a contractor.
• Work with the contractor to design the addition and draw up all specifications.
• Arrange for financing.
• Contractor will build the addition, but your contract will state what labor you are to do.

Doing your "homework"

Once you've decided to add on, consider the timing. You don't want a project that's going to be stalled by a fierce winter (though interior finishing work can be done in bad weather). If you have a costly and complicated plan, you might want to consider adding on in stages over a longer period of time — a 3-year remodeling plan, for instance — instead of doing it all at once.

Also, you must decide whether you or a professional will design the addition. Whatever your decision, some preliminary work must be done — necessary work if you design the addition yourself, optional work if you have a professional prepare the design. For some, this "homework" can help make a better-informed partner in the process; to others it may seem superfluous or redundant, since it's the kind of thing professionals can do quickly—and will do whether you've done it or not. Some architects, designers, and contractors say they like to work with homeowners who've done some of the preliminaries, because these clients will better understand the project from the beginning. Most say they don't really expect clients to do much along this line, and don't mind working with them from scratch.

Learn about your present house. To begin, gather all the pertinent facts about your existing house. Study its structure. Find which are the bearing walls (the ones that support the roof) — any addition that involves removal of all or part of a bearing wall adds to the expense. Determine the width and depth of your foundation—go into the basement or crawl space and measure. If you want a second-story addition, your foundation must be able to support it or you'll have to put in a new foundation. The building inspector will give you the necessary specifications.

Learn where all the plumbing is — supply pipes and drain pipes—you can trace their locations in the basement. Note where the water enters the house from the street main, and where the large drain pipe leaves the house to connect with the public sewer or septic tank. The farther away from existing plumbing a new bathroom or other room requiring plumbing fixtures is, the more complicated and expensive installation will be.

Measure your rooms. Measure your lot. How many feet from structure to property lines? From structure to street? From house to detached garage? These are all-important zoning considerations. Once you've gathered all the necessary information, collect it on a fact sheet and use it to make a scale drawing of your house and lot. Be sure to indicate plumbing outlets. To sum up, have as thorough a grasp of the existing situation as possible.

What do you really want? Next, you start thinking about what you want to add on. Remember, there are any number of possibilities to consider. It may not be so simple as saying, "We need a new bedroom, so we'll add a bedroom." You might want to think about adding a new kitchen, changing the present kitchen into a family room, and making the present family room into a new master bedroom. Or the garage may become the new bedroom you need, so that the present master bedroom, with its good light, can become a pottery studio.

What are the uses of the addition? Next you should enumerate all the purposes you want the addition to serve. Say you want a new family room. What, specifically, should it include? Space for

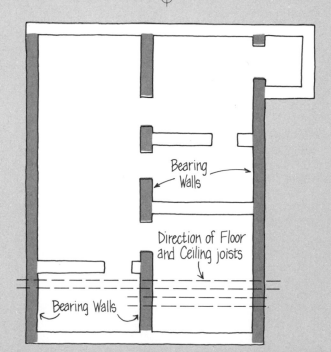

Bearing walls help support house's structure. Removing them is more involved than changing nonbearing walls.

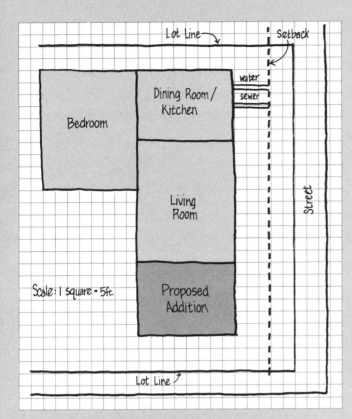

Preliminary sketches you do yourself need not be precise. Aim is to try out many possibilities.

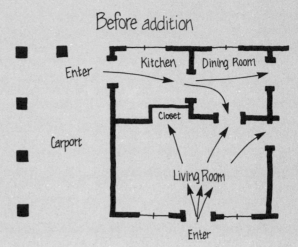

Before addition, traffic flows through centers of rooms, disrupting other family activities.

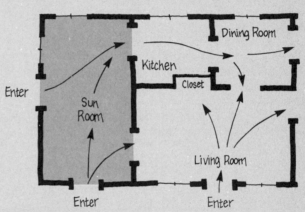

Addition's badly situated doors fail to rectify poor traffic flow through the rooms.

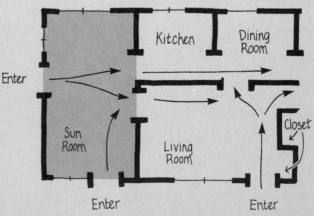

Same addition: different door placement channels traffic flow along sides of rooms out of activity areas.

games? For TV? For storage? For entertaining? For dining? If you plan a new master bedroom, what view should it have? Do you want more or less privacy than you have now? Do you want morning or afternoon sun? Do you want the bedroom to adjoin an existing bathroom, or will you build a new one?

Consider the traffic patterns in the new room and the effect of the room on traffic patterns throughout the rest of the house. Keep in mind that traffic should generally stay close to walls rather than run through the center of a room.

Get all the members of the family together and discuss everybody's ideas. Get a pad of graph paper, sharpen a jarful of pencils, and begin fiddling around with the possibilities.

Thinking about design. Besides your study of space and its uses, you'll want to begin giving serious thought to design. This gets into the area of esthetic taste and judgment; no absolute standards prevail. Some people want their room addition to blend so completely with the existing house that there's no telling where one stops and the other begins. Others don't mind a contrasting addition, so long as it harmonizes with the existing structure's colors, shapes, and textures in ways that are not extreme. Still others prefer boldness and build additions with no style similarities whatever to the existing house. Carried to its extremes, this is known as "collision architecture"; it obviously takes a great deal of flair to carry off.

When developing ideas for space usage and design, remember that your first idea is rarely your best one. Explore in one direction, then leave it behind and go in an entirely different way. Do this as many times as possible; you're bound to make new, pertinent, and helpful discoveries.

Zoning ordinances and building codes

Every community has zoning ordinances and building codes to protect standards of health, safety, and land use. Any addition to your house must comply with these standards. Compliance is monitored in two ways: your building plans must be approved by officials before you can begin work, and the work in progress will be inspected periodically.

If you hire an architect or building designer to design your addition and a general contractor to build it, you may never have to come in contact with the building inspector or the planning commission—except, perhaps, to make some inquiries in the preliminary planning stages. The professionals working for you will take care of satisfying all zoning and code requirements and getting all necessary permits and inspections. If you do all the work yourself, of course, you will need to deal directly with the building department and the planning office.

Yet even if you plan to have everything done by professionals, familiarizing yourself with zoning restrictions and building codes can help you in the early planning stages, before you call in the architect or contractor. If you take rough plans to a building inspector you can learn whether they violate ordinances or codes, and if they do, you will probably get some suggestions about how to bring them into conformity.

Zoning ordinances regulate land use. Designed to regulate community land use, zoning ordinances may affect your proposed addition. In general, they separate commercial, industrial, and residential areas, establishing boundaries to prevent business from migrating into residential neighborhoods. Zoning ordinances regulate land use *within* each area, too. Regulations apply largely to the exterior and location of stuctures, but they also apply to the way the property is used, such as for business or rental purposes. Sections of the zoning ordinances pertaining to residential zones regulate the following:

• Occupancy—the number of persons unrelated by blood or marriage who may live in a dwelling.
• Commercial use — businesses such as garages, stores, breeding kennels, and commercial stables are banned, but some professional offices may be allowed.
• Height of buildings.
• Distances between structure and property lines.
• Percentage of lot covered by structure.
• Parking requirements.
• Architectural amenities.

Your addition and zoning ordinances. Here are several questions relating to zoning ordinances that you should consider when planning your addition:

• Will the house with the addition occupy a greater percentage of the lot than is permitted under the

Convert garage to an apartment? Zoning approval likely if there are no cooking fixtures and it meets code on ventilation, windows.

Add a second story? Permissible if it doesn't exceed height limits and is all right with neighbors.

Replace garage with carport? Make sure it doesn't encroach on setback limit measured from surveyed property line, not from edge of sidewalk.

Fence higher than 6 feet? Variance needed.

Extend house? Area may exceed total lot coverage permitted under zoning. Apply for a variance.

Build closer to property line? In most areas, if closer than 5 feet, a variance is needed; if closer than 3 feet, code requires solid fire wall, no windows or doors.

Six ways a house can grow

Which way is best for you?

When you first begin to think of adding on, you'll want to explore a large number of alternatives. Never settle for the first or most obvious plan—at least not until you've considered many possibilities. The kind of addition you finally construct depends, of course, on many factors: What are the zoning restrictions? What type of lot do you have—is it a flat piece of ground? Is it a steep hillside? What is the configuration of your present structure? Of equal importance are design considerations and the purposes you want the addition to serve.

The six ideas on this page are meant to give you some notion of various types of additions you can consider. Rather than being exact, detailed designs, they are merely suggestions of the kinds of additions that are possible and that have been done.

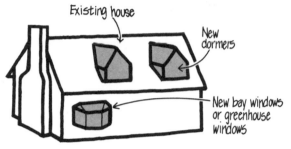

Add space by pushing out windows

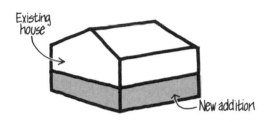

Add a full basement

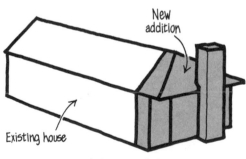

Extend front of house

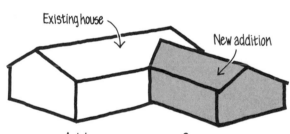

Add room on new footing

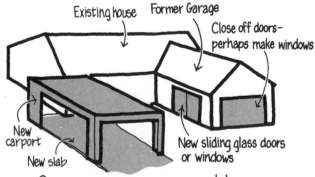

Convert garage to a usable room

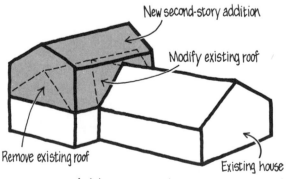

Add a second story

ordinance (usually 50 percent, but sometimes as little as 25 percent)?

• Will the boundary wall of the addition come closer to the side lot boundary than the permitted distance (typically 5 feet)?

• If the addition involves adding a second story, will it extend the roof crest above the height limit for your zone?

• Are you required to have covered, off-street parking? If you convert your garage to living quarters, will you have enough room on your lot to accommodate the displaced cars?

• Will an addition to the front of the house come too close to the street-side property line? (One of the most common miscalculations homeowners make is to consider the front sidewalk as the street boundary of their property. In many communities the front property line is actually a few feet back from the sidewalk. Before you launch a project that involves adding on to the front of the house, check your plot plan—available at the tax assessor's office—to find out just where your street-side boundary actually runs.)

Obtaining a zoning variance. If your proposed addition violates the zoning ordinance, what can you do? You may have a good reason for wishing to deviate from zoning requirements. Your house may have been built at a time when 3 feet was the commonly accepted minimum distance between house and side boundary. Your subdivision may have been replotted after the house was built, making your lot smaller now than it was originally, so that even the most modest addition may exceed the minimum area requirements — yet your family has outgrown the house and you don't want to move. In short, you may have compelling reasons for deviating from the zoning laws.

If you do, your first step is to apply for a variance. (If a professional is designing your addition, he or she will work with you throughout the variance process.) You might be granted a variance if you can prove that strict application of the rules would result in "practical difficulties or undue hardship." (It's always good, by the way, to couch your variance request in phrases used in the part of the ordinance that describes variances—phrases such as "undue hardship.") The procedure for obtaining a variance involves several steps:

1. Fill in an application for a variance. The form is available from the building department or zoning office; a filing fee is usually required.

2. If the variance you request is a minor one — involving, say, only a few inches' deviation — you may get an "administrative variance." If the variance involves substantial change, it will probably be reviewed by a special panel of experts.

3. Your petition will be reviewed in a public hearing. Any decision, whether it is in your favor or not,

can be appealed within a given number of days.

4. You can appeal an unfavorable decision to the appropriate legislative body—city council, board of supervisors, or whatever — for a public hearing on the issue.

5. Appeal of the appeal is a possibility — but a remote one. It's a matter for the courts and can cost a lot of time and money.

An approved variance is usually valid for 1 year. If you haven't completed the addition within that time, you must reapply. However, building inspectors can certify that work is in progress and extend the deadline.

Building codes regulate construction. Building codes are concerned principally with construction practices—with structural design and strength and durability of building materials. The codes state what you can and cannot do in erecting a structure. For example, codes regulate the square footage of bedrooms, the area of windows in habitable rooms, and similar matters. In addition, they regulate specifications for foundations, framing, electrical wiring, and plumbing. Properly enforced, building codes ensure that steel is actually inside the foundations, that spans are within limits so floors won't sag, that walls are properly braced and nailed, and so on. Usually you can obtain excerpts of the regulations that apply to your particular situation from the building department at city hall at little or no cost.

In some situations, particularly if you're adding on to an older home, strict application of the building code could require you to bring the entire house up to the present code. This is almost always the case if the cost of the addition totals more than 50 percent of the present market value of the house, excluding the lot.

If a proposed addition doesn't conform to the building code, it may still be approved. The head of the building department has the authority to permit suitable alternatives, provided they do not weaken the structure, endanger the safety or security of the occupants, or violate the property rights of neighbors.

In some instances your proposed addition might require review by an architectural review board. This normally happens only when the design is so unusual that the building inspector or other official feels that it warrants closer scrutiny by a body of professionals.

Choosing an architect

Your home is an expression of your family's identity. Adding rooms to your home, then, is more than just a construction project; it's a personal project. In choosing an architect, you'll want to find one who is not only technically and artistically skilled, but one with whom you and your family feel comfortable and compatible. You don't want an architect who will haughtily ignore your ideas and impose his or her own standards. You do want one who will take your ideas seriously, add his or her own knowledge, skill, judgment, and taste, and come up with a design that will make you say, "This is exactly what I wanted."

Of course, you can't always tell beforehand how well any given architect will work for you, but if you're concerned about a good working relationship with an architect, you can direct your attention to that subject as well as technical ones when you're choosing.

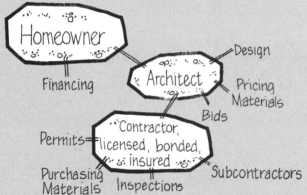

If you hire an architect to design your addition and monitor construction to completion, you'll pay more but have relatively few details to handle.

Architect or building designer?

An architect is a professional who is licensed to practice by the state. An architect's training includes education in design from the esthetic, functional, and engineering points of view. To get a license, an architect must pass a rigorous examination.

A building designer isn't licensed by the state. There is a professional organization, however — the American Institute of Building Designers — that helps set and regulate standards for the profession. Building designers generally don't have engineering expertise; they focus on the esthetic and functional components of design. So, when preparing finished plans, they normally consult with engineers.

Besides designing your addition for you, either of these professionals can help in the selection of a contractor, and can administer the contract that you and the contractor sign. Essentially, this means that the architect or building designer will monitor construction and help control the quality of the work.

How to find an architect

To find an architect or building designer, you can call the nearest office of the American Institute of Archi-tects (though not all practicing architects belong to the AIA) or the nearest office of the American Institute of Building Designers. The building editor or real estate editor of the local newspaper may be helpful, as may real estate brokers. Neighbors and friends who have worked with such professionals are often a good reference source.

Once you have located some architects or designers, you can arrange a meeting with each one to discuss your plans and needs, and to look at some of the professional's building plans and photos of finished projects. Ask for the names and addresses of other clients and request permission to call them. Be strong in expressing your concern for a good working relationship, and in general try to determine whether you'd be happy working with the person.

After you've done some shopping, think things over carefully and make your choice. Once you've decided and have agreed to employ a particular architect or designer, the next meeting should be in your home, where the architect's work (and charges) will begin.

Architects' fees and rates

Your architect can design the structure, provide working drawings and specifications, and then leave the construction or supervision of construction up to you. Or, the architect can do everything from designing through monitoring construction. Generally, architects don't like to "let go" of their work before it's fully completed; they like to make certain that their designs are correctly realized by the builder. Obviously, contract administration by an architect removes a big burden from the homeowner, and, obviously, it increases the architect's bill.

It's important that the architect or designer know your working budget from the beginning, and that the planned addition stay within your stated limits. It does no good to have a spectacular set of plans for an addition you can't afford to build.

You and your architect will agree at the beginning of the project on the type and method of payment. You can choose from a variety of payment methods, ranging from a flat fee to a percentage of the entire project's cost. For simple consultation, architects usually charge hourly rates, anywhere from $20 to $50 or more per hour. For drawing up plans and specifications, architects may charge an hourly fee or a flat fee, agreed upon at the beginning. For a project in which the architect supervises construction, the customary fee runs 15 to 25 percent of total construction costs.

Other fee arrangements may be possible as well, depending on the architect. For instance, some may combine an hourly fee for a certain part of the project with a flat fee for another part. The final details must be worked out between you and your architect.

Fees and fee arrangements with building designers are similar to those for architects.

Choosing a contractor

A general contractor is a professional builder, licensed by the state, whose responsibility is the actual building of a structure. Contractors normally employ a number of laborers and craftsmen, such as carpenters, and arrange for other work, such as plumbing and wiring, to be done by subcontractors on a project-by-project basis.

If your architect is monitoring the construction of your addition, he or she will be instrumental in hiring the general contractor to do the work (subject, of course, to your approval). If you are to supervise the work, you'll have to find the contractor yourself.

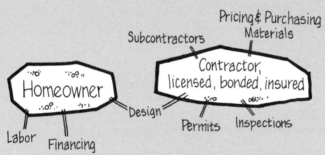

Building a simple addition, you can save architect's fees, collaborate with contractor on design, and do some of the construction labor yourself.

Finding a contractor

You can get the names of contractor firms from architects and building designers, from friends, from trade associations, or from material suppliers. Call the firms you've been referred to and ask for the names of some of their past clients; then talk to those clients about the contractors and arrange to see their work.

On the basis of that procedure, select two or three promising firms. Ask them for names of material suppliers and subcontractors and bank and credit references; check these to learn the financial condition of the firm. Contractors are accustomed to providing such information and should give you these references willingly. You can also call your local Better Business Bureau to find out if there have been any complaints filed against a contractor.

In addition, verify the validity of contractors' licenses with the state licensing agency, and check their public liability and property damage insurance with their insurance carriers.

How to get contractor bids

Submit your plans and specifications to two or three contractors for bids. The list of specifications should be as detailed as possible, including all materials, model numbers, types of fixtures, colors, paints and stains, electrical switch covers, moldings, doorknobs, and so forth.

You may not always choose the least expensive bid; you may be willing to pay more for certain pluses, such as higher-quality workmanship or a more amicable relationship with the contractor. Even so, bids are the chief consideration for most homeowners.

Drawing up a contract

Once you've accepted a bid, you and the contractor will draw up a written contract based on that bid. As the working agreement between the two of you, the contract is a very important document — you can refer to it if any differences arise. Therefore it's important to make the contract as detailed as possible.

Construction materials. The contract should list all materials to be used in construction. It should be thoroughly detailed, itemizing all materials and fixtures, even things that may seem insignificant, such as drawer pulls and cabinet hinges. If any disagreements arise about materials, you and your contractor can refer to this list of agreed-upon specifications. Anything not included in the contract and added later will increase your cost.

Time schedule. You and your contractor will include in the contract a time schedule for the project — a beginning date and a completion date. The contractor obviously can't be responsible for delays caused by strikes or material shortages. You have no effective legal way to enforce a schedule even though it's written into the contract. Your best leverage is a good working relationship with the contractor—and the stipulation that the final payment will be withheld until the work is completed.

Site preparation and cleanup. Your building site may need to be prepared for construction: fences and shrubs removed, concrete torn up, land graded. If you expect the contractor to do this, you must include it in the contract.

As a job progresses, and once it's finished, there will be a lot of debris on the site, and disposing of it usually is no easy matter. Again, if you expect the contractor to clean up, it must be in the contract.

Method of payment. Payment, of course, is covered in the contract as well. Usually payment is made in installments as the work progresses, or with an initial payment at the beginning of the project and the balance at the project's completion. You should withhold the final payment until after the lien period has expired and until final repairs and adjustments have been made. If you have secured outside financing, the financing agency may hold its final payment until the lien period has expired.

Protection against liens. Under the laws of most states, anyone who performs labor or supplies materials for a building can file a lien against the building if he or she is not paid. If the contractor doesn't settle the claim, the building's owner may be liable. There are various ways to protect yourself against this eventuality: you can pay suppliers of material and labor directly; you can require evidence of such payment from the contractor before making each progress payment and the final payment; or you can require the contractor to post a bond of sufficient size specifically to protect your property. This bond would be in addition to the one required by the state from a licensed contractor — that minimum bond might not be large enough to cover all claims against a contractor if he or she defaulted.

To be valid, liens must be filed within a specified time after construction is completed, and the time limit that a lien remains in effect is also specified by law. If you are selling your property during this period, the settlement of valid liens by payment or legal action will be required before title is transferred.

The laws covering liens vary from state to state, so you should consult an attorney before entering into any contract for work on your property.

Working with a contractor

In the course of a room-addition project, it's normal for problems to arise. Don't be dismayed by disagreements you might have with your contractor. Clearly, he or she won't have the same personal attachment to the project that you do. You'll be anxious that the new addition live up to your dreams of it, and you're likely to be a bit edgy having all those workers around your house for what can seem like years. And your understandable nervousness can magnify any difficulties.

Once the project gets going, keep a close eye on the work and the materials being used. Feel free to ask questions — it's your house and your money — but try not to get in the way of the work. And you should try to be around home at least some part of every day so the contractor can ask you questions. Don't give any direct instructions to the contractor's employees or to subcontractors; always deal directly with the contractor.

After the job is completed, you should address a formal letter of acceptance to the contractor, who then files a completion notice with the county recorder's office.

If you plan to hire a contractor but do some of the work yourself, be sure to check for any objections to your presence on the job. In strongly unionized communities, a union contractor might be prohibited from permitting you to do some of the work. In other circumstances it might simply be the contractor's personal policy not to work with nonprofessionals, even if they are his clients.

Some of the most common jobs homeowners do during construction include installing insulation, painting, and cleaning up. Your contractor will want to be assured that your part in the work won't delay completion of the job. Your responsibilities will be spelled out in the contract, and you'll have to sign a written statement releasing the contractor from any liability for the work you perform.

And, of course, your contract may call for the contractor to do only a limited amount of work — foundation, frame, and roof, for instance. Once that is done and the contractor has left the job, you can finish the project yourself.

Being your own contractor

Being your own general contractor means that you will be responsible for everything from obtaining permits to hiring subcontractors and laborers to arranging for building inspections. But before you do anything else, check with your insurance broker. Your standard homeowner's policy *will not* cover liability for injury to persons you employ. It is a simple matter for you to purchase a policy, known as workers' compensation insurance, to cover your liability for work-related injuries.

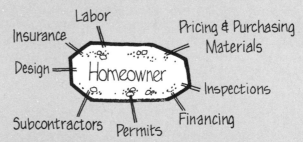

Doing everything yourself you can save money, but you'll load yourself up with a multiplicity of tasks.

Workers' compensation insurance

Though its provisions vary from state to state, workers' compensation insurance generally pays all costs of treatment — surgical, medical, and hospital — required to cure or relieve the effects of an occupational injury. It also reimburses the injured worker for wages lost while recovering from an injury. If the injury is fatal, the insurance pays burial expenses and awards survivors a settlement. Even though you carry workers' compensation insurance, you may have additional liability, particularly if you are proved negligent.

Where to get it. You can get a workers' compensation policy through your insurance broker, directly from an insurance company, or from a state fund if one is provided by your state. You can obtain a policy for 3 months, 6 months, or whatever term you think will adequately cover the duration of your project. If the work is still in progress when the policy expires, coverage can be extended.

Paying the premium. You pay for workers' compensation insurance before the work begins. The cost is figured on a combination of three factors: the estimated number of hours required to complete the task, the rates of pay for the crafts involved, and the relative personal risk inherent in the work itself. The premium for roofers is higher than for cabinetmakers, for example, because of the higher risk involved in roofing work.

After your addition is completed, you'll add up your actual payroll expense. If it exceeds your initial estimate, you'll owe the insurance carrier an additional sum. If it is less than your estimate, you may be entitled to a refund. However, there are minimum premiums, whatever your costs.

If no worker you employ directly will earn more than the minimum set by the state workers' compensation board (normally somewhere around $100), then it's possible that your homeowner's insurance will cover your liability. Check this with the state board and with your insurance company.

Make sure that workers who are employed by a subcontractor working on your addition are covered by the subcontractor's policy.

Registering as an employer. If you employ people directly and if they will earn more than the minimum amount set by the state, you must not only have a workers' compensation policy, but you must also register with the state and federal governments as an employer, withhold and remit income taxes and disability insurance, and pay social security insurance.

Hiring subcontractors

When you act as your own general contractor and put various parts of your project out to bid with subcontractors, you must use the same care you'd exercise in hiring a general contractor. You will need to check references, financial resources, and insurance coverage of a number of subcontractors, get bids, work out detailed contracts, and then carefully supervise the work. The process will be time-consuming, but you'll save money and have much more control over the quality of the work.

Shopping for money

If you're like most homeowners who add on, you'll finance your addition by arranging some kind of loan. But before making any loan arrangements you must have finished plans and specifications for your project, and accurate estimates. If you plan to do the work yourself, go to suppliers to establish the costs of all materials; otherwise, your contractor will supply this information. Next you need to determine the type of financing that best suits your needs and for which you can qualify.

What type of financing?

The type of financing that's best depends primarily on how much money you need to borrow. The chart on the facing page compares popular types of home improvement loans. Once you have a general idea how the terms of various loans relate to your personal financial situation, you can contact lending institutions.

You can borrow for home improvements from a variety of sources: commercial banks, savings and loan associations, savings banks, mortgage banks, and credit unions (not to mention rich friends or relatives).

Start with a lender where you're known, where you've done business before, such as a bank where you have a savings or checking account, or a credit union where you've financed a car. Your past or present business there may be just the right foundation for a new home improvement loan.

Besides the loan types indicated on the chart, you may also be able to finance your project by borrowing against your life insurance equity, refinancing your present mortgage, obtaining a second mortgage, getting an advance against an open-ended mortgage, or remortgaging your home if it is paid for. Check the details of these methods as they pertain to your situation.

Qualifying for a loan

To obtain a loan you'll need to file an application with a lending institution, stating the purpose of the loan and the amount needed. You'll also have to provide personal financial data that will convince the lender the loan is a good risk. Before you do that, make sure your financial situation is in order—your credit record will show whether you are a good or poor credit risk.

If possible, pay off outstanding debts, or consolidate them. And pay off charge accounts that have large balances. Remember, all debts will affect the amount of money you will be able to borrow.

Five Types of Home Improvement Loans

TYPE OF LOAN	MAXIMUM TO BORROW	REPAYMENT PERIOD	ADVANTAGES	DISADVANTAGES
Commercial loan (available from commercial bank)	Varies according to your income and credit standing	Negotiable. Usually 3 months to 1 year (may be renewable if loan is reduced or principal payments are made)	Usually an unsecured loan on borrower's signature alone. Total interest is less than for conventional home improvement bank loan, as it is calculated at simple interest. Payment of both interest and principal are negotiable. Faster to arrange; no property appraisal necessary.	Loans usually granted only to long-standing customers with excellent credit records. Shorter repayment period than for other types of loans.
Home improvement loan (available from commercial bank)	Up to 80% of equity on your home	Usually 5 years (maximum of 15 years at most banks)	Good credit standing with your own bank may enable you to bargain for an interest rate at the lower end of their scale. Longer repayment period than commercial loan.	Discount or add-on interest rather than simple interest—total interest may be more than for a shorter-term commercial loan. Total interest rate is figured on a prearranged repayment period, and early repayment is penalized. Larger loans may require bank to take a second deed of trust. Also, lender requires a property appraisal and a lot book report, totaling up to $50.
Home improvement loan (available from savings and loan association)	Usually 100% of improvement cost up to $15,000. State associations usually limit amount to $15,000 on any one property.	Usually 10 years (maximum of 15 years)	Longer repayment period than some other loans, therefore smaller monthly payments. If you already have a second mortgage on your home, a savings and loan association may be more willing than a commercial bank to make a home improvement loan.	Early repayment is penalized. On loans over a certain amount, lender usually requires a second deed of trust, property appraisal, and lot book report. Total amount of interest may be high if repayment period is long. Some savings and loan associations do not handle home improvement loans.
FHA-insured Title 1 short-term loan (available from lending institutions that participate in FHA program)	$5,000	Up to maximum of 7 years	Borrower can often obtain loan on signature alone—no cosigner needed, no securities held. Lessee (as well as home owner) can apply for loan if lease lasts longer than repayment period. Interest rate slightly lower than current commercial bank and savings and loan association rates. No prepayment penalties.	Loan may be difficult to obtain in some areas unless you belong to a participating credit union. Loan can be used only on essential improvements which make home more livable and useful—not on luxury-type improvements. They must be an integral, built-in part of house.
Home improvement loan (available from credit union)	Varies with each credit union, depending on availability of funds	Usually 5 years (maximum of 10 years for federally chartered credit unions)	Simple rather than discount interest. Usually no finance charges other than interest. No prepayment penalties.	Must be member of credit union to obtain loan. Lender may take a second deed of trust. Some require property appraisal and lot book report. Not all credit unions offer loans for home improvements.

Project Ideas for Adding Living Space to Your Home

Once they have decided to add on, most homeowners go shopping for ideas. By studying finished projects, they occasionally find an entire addition that would be just right for them. More often they discover an esthetic touch here, a functional solution there, that they'd like to incorporate into their own addition.

This section is intended as a kind of supermarket for idea shoppers. Here are the stories of many new rooms that represent a broad sample of the possibilities open to you. Our aim in selecting these additions is to present ideas that are both handsome and practical. We have also tried to choose several whose designs might be easily adapted, in whole or in part, to other circumstances.

In order to offer more than just a cursory glimpse, we present each addition in a number of ways, using photographs, floor plans, detailed drawings, three-dimensional sketches, and written descriptions. Though many of the written descriptions contain details about structure, design, or materials, the focus is on the whole rather than the parts. We are addressing the larger issue of your addition's overall design rather than offering a collection of interesting decorator touches or unusual solutions to storage, traffic, or wall covering problems. (For an abundance of tips along those lines, see the *Sunset* book *Ideas for Remodeling Your Home*). Still, that doesn't preclude the possiblity that you'll find a skylight in one house, a stairway in another, and an entryway in a third, and make them all a part of your final design.

Also included in this section of the book are special features that present ideas for cutting add-on costs, for energy conservation, for using the greenhouse concept in adding on, and for converting attics into usable rooms.

Two-story addition yields breakfast room, downstairs pantry

Upstairs, master bedroom gains walk-in closet

The owners of this house didn't feel comfortable having all their meals in the dining room. They wanted a small, informal area off the kitchen for breakfasts and for storage. And they wanted more closet space upstairs off the master bedroom. They answered their needs with a simple, unobtrusive two-story addition.

The addition blends in splendidly with the existing house, echoing its forms and materials. Since the breakfast room backs onto a hill, the owners wanted a view up as well as out; consequently, a tempered glass roof offers uphill views to azaleas and pines. And an upstairs skylight illuminates the new walk-in closet and dressing room.

It's a small addition. The downstairs portion, connected to the kitchen by an open doorway, is 7½ by 12½ feet. Two-thirds of this space is eating area; the rest is pantry and broom closet. In cool weather, air near the glass is warmed by an energy-saving draft barrier heater on a small ledge at the base of the windows.

Architect: Donald King Loomis.

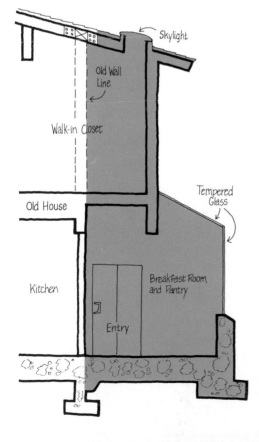

Small addition makes a big difference. Slanted glass roof, glass wall let in plenty of light. New breakfast room downstairs and walk-in closet upstairs merge perfectly with existing house.

17

Front expansion gives old home a new face

Pushing out and up adds living room, bedroom, loft

A room addition on the front of a house has two advantages: it can dramatically alter the structure's street-side appearance, and it makes use of that often-expendable area, the front lawn.

The house on this page began as a weekend retreat. New owners wanted it for a permanent family residence, but they needed more functional space and wanted to update its appearance. For them, front lawn was unimportant, so the natural place to add and accomplish both their goals was in the front.

The house received a new shed-roof addition that reaches all the way to the municipality's height limit, giving views over neighboring houses to the ocean. The roof repeats the angle of the existing house's roof, helping to tie the structures together esthetically.

Downstairs is a new bedroom that opens onto a new, fenced-in patio. The room is windowless on three sides to insulate it from street noises.

Upstairs is the new living room with its views over the rooftops. To one side is a tea-for-two loft for even more dizzying views.

Architect: John Blanton.

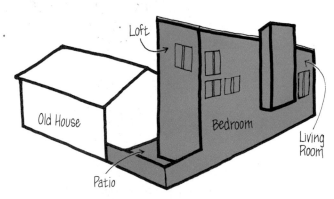

Dramatic addition gives front of plain house a brand-new look. There's drama inside, too, in sharp pitch of living-room ceiling and loft with spectacular view.

1920s home gains space, light, and a lean-to kitchen

Old kitchen becomes family dining room

The lean-to was surely one of man's earliest constructed shelters. That old basic form appears again in this new kitchen. Simple to construct, it allows a great deal of open interior space.

The main framework of the trusses that support the sloping roof is built of 2 by 6s; smaller members are 2 by 4s bolted between them. And between the 2 by 6s is a space just wide enough for recessed track lighting.

The old kitchen in this 1920s home was dark and cramped. The new kitchen has large vertical windows in the back wall and translucent glass panes in the roof to provide plenty of northern light and to give a pleasant garden view. There's plenty of space for table and chairs, as well as more than enough cabinets and maple butcher-block counter tops.

Architect: Tom Devine.

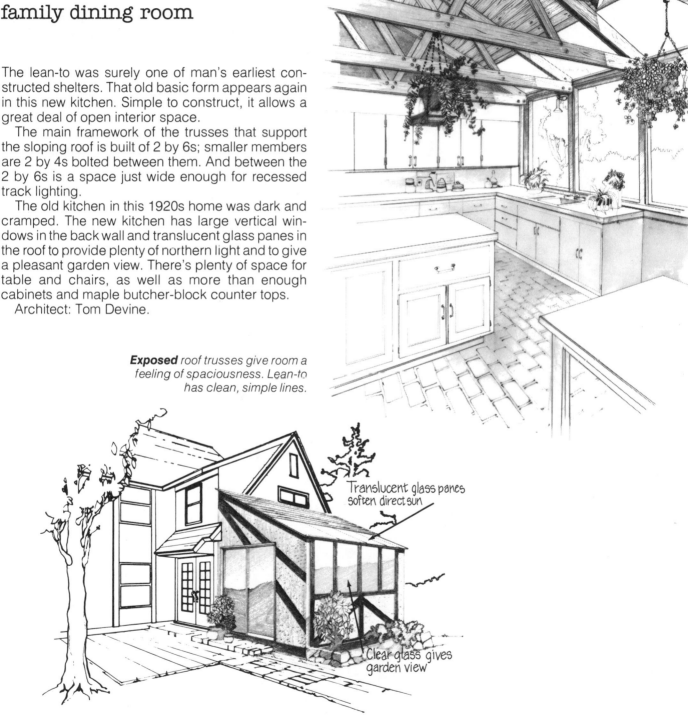

Exposed roof trusses give room a feeling of spaciousness. Lean-to has clean, simple lines.

Translucent glass panes soften direct sun

Clear glass gives garden view

Angled property line results in wedge-shaped room

Library addition gives more space for owner's book collection

Sometimes an addition takes a certain shape because of the shape of a lot. An angled lot line determined the wedge-shaped floor plan of this library room addition. The owners, both bibliophiles, needed as much wall space as they could muster to store their ever-growing collection of books; they built the room to fill as much of their side yard as setbacks would allow.

Narrow floor-to-ceiling windows bring in adequate daylight but still leave sufficient wall room for bookshelves. Skylights let in more light through the open beamed ceiling. Overhead track lights and reading lamps as well as the natural light provide illumination.

This is a quiet room — no television or radio, just yards and yards of books (which have acoustical as well as intellectual advantages: they help muffle sounds). The owners and their children use it for reading, writing, study, and quiet games. They've panelled the walls with rough-sawn cedar and made shelves of cedar 2 by 10s. Built-in file drawers along one wall are handy and unobtrusive. There is a brick fireplace at one end.

Designer: Lloyd Faulkner.

Louvered floor-to-ceiling windows

Library room *addition gets plenty of light from skylight and slim louvered windows. Built-in drawers provide ample storage.*

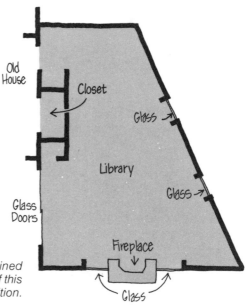

Old House

Closet

Glass

Library

Glass Doors

Fireplace

Glass

Angled *lot line determined unconventional shape of this library addition.*

New room off master bedroom is adult retreat

Owners gain quiet study facing bay and deck garden

When the couple who owned this house added on, they had two teen-age children living at home, both ardent music lovers. The parents wanted more privacy for the children and for themselves.

Their addition gave private space to everyone by expanding the living room to accommodate the teen-agers and their pursuits, and by adding a new study to the master bedroom as a quiet retreat for the parents.

An enclosed garden deck was added off the existing master bath and bedroom extension. Relaxing in bed, one can look into the garden deck on one side, or look through the study to a spectacular view of San Francisco Bay on the other side. The study was designed three steps lower than the master bedroom so the window seat would not obstruct the view.

To unite the line of study and deck, the owners pushed the master bedroom wall out 5 feet, which gave them some new walk-in closets. This extension also created a windbreak for the garden deck.

Architect: Donald King Loomis.

Beamed ceiling repeats similar one in adjoining bedroom. Behind doors, a large storage closet.

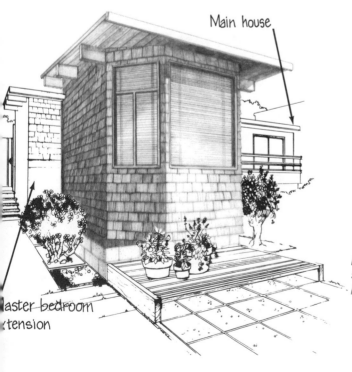

Main house

Master bedroom extension

Following existing roof line, new study blends with main house, pushes out to face the bay.

Once a deck, now a cheery study and bedrooms

Lagoon-side home gains space for private pursuits

Originally a small, cozy, seasonal cottage with excellent views of a nearby lagoon, this house had been a year-round residence for some time. When the owners wanted more private space for themselves and their children, they decided to leave the living room facing the lagoon, because it gave the house a cottagelike atmosphere.

Without changing the view side of the house they converted and extended an existing street-side deck into a study and bedrooms. Retaining the feeling of the beamed deck, they enclosed it with redwood walls and covered its beams with gray-tinted glass. Slanted slightly for water drainage, the tinted glass reduces glare. Off the study, a garage was enlarged and divided into two bedrooms, each with a window seat.

To discourage traffic through the living room and to add to the feeling of privacy, a new entry with storage closets was added between the carport and the study.

Architect: Donald King Loomis.

Large study has window seat, beamed ceiling. Light panels recessed in ceiling beams supplement natural light.

Once a solarium, now a family entertainment area

Materials salvaged from original house used in addition

This lovely old 1905 house had a more-than-ample formal living room for entertaining, but it lacked a good place for the family's four children and their friends to spend time (there are always lots of young people using the tennis court in the backyard). To keep tennis balls out of the living room, the owners expanded a small solarium into a large, informal rumpus room for the young set.

The finished room works well for the entire family. Both parents and children do a lot of entertaining; the adults in the living room and the young people in the rumpus room can enjoy privacy simultaneously.

The addition uses doors, beams, and shingles that retain the traditional character of the house. Carpenters saved as many materials as possible when they removed an exterior wall, and used them to finish off the new exterior. Inside, the beams from the ceiling of the adjoining living room are reiterated in the new room.

Architect: James Mount.

rumpus
receives
light

Rumpus room addition contains plenty of space for visiting with friends, bumper pool, and a relatively quiet game of chess.

Present blends with past in ranch house addition

Doubling in size, weekend country home becomes more formal retreat

Comfort *exudes from new living room. Wood rafters add structural depth, counterpoint with flat wall surfaces.*

New deck off end of living room

Built-in *window seat offers a quiet reading area facing a stand of redwood trees.*

With an eye to making it a permanent residence someday, the owners of this century-old ranch house added on without sacrificing the traditional exterior appearance they liked so much.

Extending the gabled roof northward, the addition doubles the size of the original house. To change the interior's closed-in character, a large living room extends out into the redwood trees. This new room opens up the kitchen and dining areas; its windows and skylight bring them more light and a more spacious feeling. The whole addition then appears almost large enough to be considered "grand," but its simple clean lines and materials keep it from becoming cold and aloof. The exposed wood rafters are painted with a special paint that reflects light throughout the day so as to visually animate room space.

On a lower level, an extra bedroom, playroom, and storage area were added to accommodate weekend guests.

Finally, to take fullest advantage of the beautiful setting, a new deck was added on three sides of the house. It's shaded from direct afternoon sun by the nearby big trees. The end result is a blending of nature with architecture, and past with present, giving a wonderful simplicity.

Architect: William Turnbull, MLTW/Turnbull Associates.

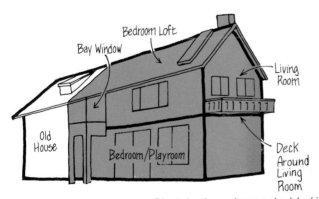

Sketch shows house doubled in size. ***Top right:*** *New spacious feeling created by merging dining, living, and kitchen areas.* ***Right:*** *Kitchen pass-through brings cook into the conversation.*

New art gallery/ entertainment area retains outdoor view

Angled windows and clerestory admit soft light

Originally this house had a living room window wall looking out to a garden and the heavily forested hills rolling off for miles beyond. The owners, avid art collectors, wanted a room for the proper display of their extensive collection of paintings, sculpture, and other art objects.

The result was a step-down gallery room off the living room where the window wall had been. Through the use of tall, angled windows the room retains much, though not all, of its original view of garden and hills, and still has an enormous amount of wall space for the display of art works. Clerestory and angled windows also create reflected light instead of direct light — important because the windows face west, and strong direct sunlight can damage art works.

The gallery is somewhat darker than the rest of the house. Floors are of oak; walls have a Japanese fabric covering; display cases are walnut, lighted indirectly from within. The lighting system combines indirect fixtures in coves with wall washers and adjustable spots on dimmers to provide complete flexibility both in display lighting and general illumination.

Since the new gallery is directly off the living room, it also serves as an entertaining area for large parties. Guests flow naturally into this space to enjoy the art and the garden view.

Architect: Lorenzo Tedesco.

This room was built for art. Shelves display objects from all over the world. Angled wall sections create discreet viewing areas.

Greenhouse idea adds light to living room

1914 house gains a new ambience and more space for plants

After buying this stately 1914 house, the owners faced three major problems: they needed more light in the living room than the existing windows provided; they wanted easier access to a basement recreation area; and they needed a larger and better location to house their growing collection of plants. All three problems were solved in a single addition—a greenhouse room.

Originally the living room ran the full length of the house's north side. Little light came in from the tree-shaded windows, and there were no windows at all on the west side. The addition opened up the west wall into a greenhouse room. Tearing out the old stairway wall leading to the basement, the owners situated the new room a few steps down from the living room. Spanning the width of the living room, it floods that room with light. The greenhouse room also acts as a landing for a new stairway leading to the basement, establishing it as a recreation area.

Besides providing an ideal indoor environment for plants, the greenhouse room creates a pleasant new focus for the entire house. It faces west—not always the best exposure in a sunny climate, but fine for an overcast one. Flanked on the west by large trees and a neighbor's house, the new room is sheltered from direct sunlight.

Architect: Gary Sortun.

Insulated glass cuts heat loss

Stairway down from main floor

View from stairway reveals plants basking in light. **Left:** Sketch shows addition's relationship to main house.

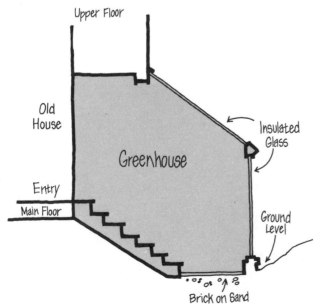

Upper Floor

Old House

Entry

Main Floor

Greenhouse

Insulated Glass

Ground Level

Brick on Sand

The greenhouse idea

Natural light and green living space

In home additions, applying the greenhouse idea to rooms you can live in has increasing appeal. "Seldom," states one architect, "do people want to live in a working greenhouse, a place cluttered with soil and propagating tools, but rather people seek the greenhouse idea as an inexpensive means to integrate light and green living space into their homes."

The benefits are many

Older homes often have dark corners and dimly lighted corridors. In many cases a greenhouse type of addition can help relieve a somber interior, opening a home to new views and bringing the feeling of the outdoors inside.

Because greenhouse rooms are flooded with light, they are a good add-on idea in geographical areas with many overcast days. The more natural light, the more benefit from natural solar energy. And with the many materials available in glass, glass coatings, shades, and ventilation, homeowners in warm climates can benefit from greenhouse rooms on east, south, or west-facing walls.

Recently architects have been considering the greenhouse idea as a passive solar heating system for major remodels. For information on solar greenhouses, consult *Sunset Homeowner's Guide to Solar Heating*.

But watch out for . . .

You should be aware of some potential gremlins in greenhouse additions. Unless properly constructed, such a room may be plagued by drafts. Applying weatherstripping to windows and doors and sealing with caulking or flashing where the new structure meets the original house should minimize air filtration. At the same time, though, proper ventilation is necessary to prevent condensation.

Direct sunlight may discolor upholstery, fade rugs, and dry out wood floors. It can also cause excessive heat buildup. To control the sun's effects, use roll-up shades of bamboo, fabric, vinyl, or aluminum, inside or outside. Reflective films can reduce the sun's glare by up to 80 percent. Perhaps the biggest challenge in adding greenhouse rooms is preventing water leaks. Always apply caulking where the greenhouse room joins the existing structure, and overlap the joint with flashing.

To locate construction suppliers, check under "Greenhouse Builders" in the Yellow Pages of the telephone directory. But even before you order materials, be sure to obtain a building permit, since some codes restrict the use of greenhouse sections in house construction.

Slant-wall *greenhouse sections convert open deck into studio. Designer: Jack Comey.*

Greenhouse sections create dining area between kitchen and storage area. Architect: Clement Chen.

Curved greenhouse sections capture sun's warmth on overcast days. Architect: Stuart Goforth.

Studio-greenhouse addition sits above entryway with view of trees.

A room for dining, a gallery for displaying art

High windows and narrow skylight admit natural light

A room addition that doesn't try to hide its identity, this dining room/gallery was built to house favorite pieces of the owners' art collection, as well as to add excitement and space to a modest colonial residence.

The new room was added to the rear of the square brick house. The exterior wall of the original house is now an interior wall of the new room — it was kept intact except for a large rectangular opening that gives visual access to the bright, art-filled room from many places in the house.

Generous high windows and a narrow skylight down the center of the slanting roof admit natural light to all areas of the high room. Mounted on a ceiling track, sliding spotlights adjust to illuminate paintings and sculptures. The flooring is black slate coated with polyurethane.

Architect: Hugh Newell Jacobsen.

Exterior wall of existing house

Inside, *new slate-floored room is bright, spacious, with plenty of wall space for paintings.*

Existing house

Brick repeats siding of existing house

Former "cracker box" house now has ample room

Expansion yields larger kitchen, entertainment area, open space

When the owners first purchased it, this 1930s house was poorly laid out, divided into many small rooms. None of the rooms took advantage of the spectacular westward view, overlooking a lake and a major city. The kitchen was dark and lacked an eating area; a long, narrow dining room obstructed traffic flow from the living room to the kitchen; and the upstairs bedrooms were dark and cramped. The owners needed more light and open space. In addition, they wanted the house to offer a multitude of environments, from an everyday kitchen to a gallery and sitting area.

Their addition redesigned interior spaces entirely and added onto the house's three levels. It pushed out the kitchen's west wall about 8 feet, extending a new bay window with an abundance of glass. This new bay became a breakfast area and focal point for the kitchen. Windows angled at 45° created an almost panoramic view, allowing the breakfaster to gaze both north and southwest.

The owners also wanted to free the dining room of its narrow, locked-in feeling. Again they pushed out, breaking up the exterior wall with a two-story window wall that reveals a breathtaking view. Not only does the new space allow for pleasant dining, but enough room is left over for an informal gallery/sitting area. This space creates a solarium for plants and insulates the quiet living room from the busy view.

Though the project added but little square footage upstairs, it eliminated what was the master bedroom suite's exterior wall. The bedroom was opened further by an interior balcony overlooking the tall dining room space and the two-story window wall.

Architect: Gary Sortun.

Above: *Small but light and airy breakfast nook.* **Below:** *Spectacular two-story window wall.*

Addition freed cramped kitchen, dining room spaces. Large windows face spectacular views.

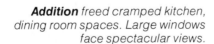
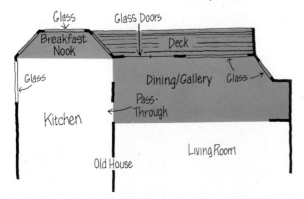

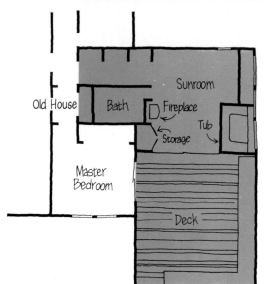

Old House

Bath

Sunroom

Fireplace

Tub

Storage

Master Bedroom

Deck

Gained: Room for relaxation, access to the outdoors

Adding a cozy study opens shady end of house to sun

New large deck adjoins both the added sunroom and the new master bedroom.

Brick fireplace, wood floor, rough fir walls and ceiling create "natural" feeling.

As an addition to a very old farmhouse, this pleasant room brings in the sun's light and warmth and provides a sense of openness as well as easy access to the outdoors.

All year around, the sunroom is at a comfortable temperature: a large oak tree and one wall of sliding glass doors keep it cool in summer. In winter, most of the heat comes from the sun through windows and acrylic skylights. The room has a wood-burning fireplace and electric heat if needed; when unoccupied it can be closed off from the rest of the house to save fuel.

The addition also includes a half bath and a sunken tub where the owners can soak and look out into the surrounding trees. Adjoining the sunroom is a new deck with built-in seating along two sides.

Building materials create attractive contrasts: Alaskan yellow cedar for the deck and benches, redwood for exterior walls, Douglas fir for interior walls and peaked ceiling, random-width white oak for the floor, earth-tone tiles around the sunken tub, and cedar lining for the closets.

Architect: Sandra Miller. Landscape designer: Michael Wills.

Abundance of windows, wood, ceramic tile, houseplants, casual furnishings help create feeling merging indoors and outdoors.

They wanted more room and a look at the waterfront

They got a bedroom suite, a living room, and a superb view

This house started out as a modest, boxy structure that didn't begin to take full advantage of views of the nearby waterfront. The owners wanted more room, more interesting interior spaces, and big chunks of the dramatic view.

The house is built on a steep lot, so the architect designed up instead of out, adding a new floor at the former roof height and redesigning the inside of the existing house. In the new middle level (formerly the top) the bedroom stayed, the kitchen and rear deck were enlarged, and the living room became a dining room. The new upper level has a master bedroom suite and a living room that opens up fully to the waterfront and mountain. The living room not only shares a two-story window wall with the middle level but also overlooks the dining room through an open well—creating real spatial drama.

The house's exterior got a completely new, decidedly updated look. It was newly sided with cedar; exterior openings remained in the same locations as before. A sloped ramp replaces the steep trail that used to lead from street to entrance.

Architect: L. Jane Hastings.

Above: *Railing rims dining room overlook; windows afford great views.* **Below:** *New look is bold but not flashy.*

Brand-new third floor includes a new bridge entrance and a balcony overlooking the dining room below.

Third-Floor Plan

Facelift for old house gives clean, contemporary look

Owners gain living room and covered entry

More living space and a cleaner, more contemporary look were goals of the owners of this house, which formerly had a fairy-tale façade of arches, dormer windows, and balconies. Adding a new entrance and living room and simplifying exterior lines met both requirements.

The existing 13 by 15-foot living room became a spacious new dining room. The arches, dormers, and balconies were removed to make room for the new covered entry and the new 16 by 24-foot living room.

Clear 1 by 10 tongue-and-groove cedar siding covers the blank exterior wall facing the street. The roofline that starts at the top of this wall rises to 15 feet in height, providing plenty of interior wall space for the family's collection of contemporary prints, paintings, and sculpture.

Interior walls are finished with 4-foot-wide panels of vinyl-covered gypsum wallboard. Clear strips of 1 by 4 redwood accent the sloping ceilings. Sliding glass doors and high jalousie windows open onto a back garden patio.

Architect: Brian Webb.

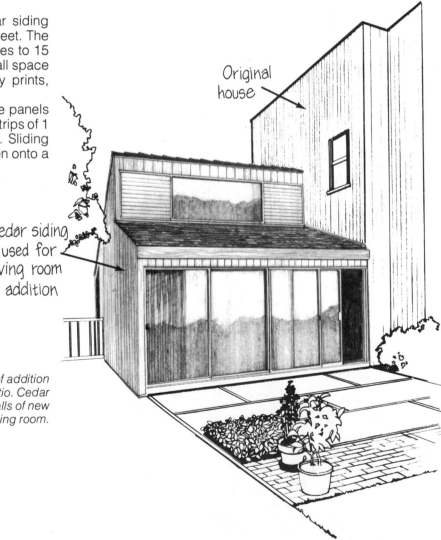

Original house

Cedar siding used for living room addition

Sliding glass doors of addition open onto inner patio. Cedar siding covers exterior walls of new living room.

Bland turned beautiful

Space between house and carport becomes new entry, bedroom, study

When the owners of this house first bought it, it was, in their words, "nondescript, but in a good location." They wanted something they could do a lot with.

Their addition wrought dramatic changes in the 40-year-old structure, situated on a narrow lot. Between the old house and the old carport they built a tall wooden box, windowless to the street, containing a new entry, bedroom, and study. The addition's bare, street-side façade hides the old structure and gives privacy. It also deliberately conceals what's inside — a varied collection of plants, rugs, contemporary furniture, and small artifacts that fills every room.

The new entry corridor, with high, skylight ceiling, leads past rows of plants to the old entry hall — now the central hub of the house. Here the wall opening between the old entry and the living room was enlarged.

The small, square study addition has a skylight along one side. From the study, a stairwell against the facade wall leads upstairs to the tall new bedroom.

The new interior spaces have an interesting and varied feel because of different sizes, ceiling heights, and window placements. Openings between rooms were enlarged to give contrastingly deep views from one room into another and to the outdoors. For instance, it's about 55 feet from the front door to the window wall at the rear of the house; the view from the entry extends through three rooms.

Architect: William Turnbull, MLTW/Turnbull Associates.

Above: At entrance to den and study, second-story skylight illuminates display shelves. **Below:** Windowless façade ensures privacy from street.

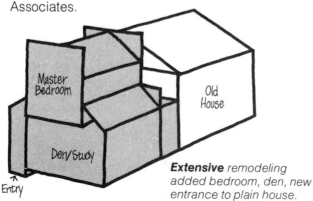

Extensive remodeling added bedroom, den, new entrance to plain house.

Skylight ceiling and glass doors flood new tile-floored entry area with light.

A natural extension of the older structure

New library/guest room harmonizes with rest of house

The owners of this house wanted a library, but they also needed a room for overnight guests. The addition they built is such a natural extension of the older structure that it doesn't appear to be an addition at all.

The owners designed the addition themselves, with the help and advice of the builder. The new library/guest room extends a bay window out into the backyard—a bay that matches one on the opposite side of the house. Inside are built-in bookcases and a window seat. At both ends of the room, built-in seats convert to single beds.

To match the line of the old house with the added room, the walls of the master bedroom and an adjoining bedroom were pushed out. The new space off the master bedroom became a small study.

Before the new addition, the back patio could be reached only through a child's bedroom. Along with the new room, the owners added a new hallway and a new rear entry for easier access to the backyard.

During construction, as many materials as possible were saved from the removed portions of exterior wall and roof; these were used on the new exterior. Recycled doors and windows became part of the addition, too.

Builder: David French.

Bay window in new room matches one on other side of house. Inside, built-in seat is also bed with storage underneath.

Old House

Library/Guest Room

Previously the kitchen of this house was too cramped for the owners. And it didn't take advantage of the view of a nearby valley and adjacent large trees. In addition to a roomier kitchen and an enhanced view, the owners wanted a space for family acitivities, reading, games, conversation, and study.

The addition shown here maintained the flavor of the existing structure. The kitchen grew out, continuing the slope of the existing roof and the beamed ceiling of the existing kitchen. Custom-made floor tiles matched the new floor with the old. The walls of the newly enlarged room are finished in resawn redwood siding and painted white. Large windows provide an excellent north view where none existed before. The slope of the ceiling gives a sense of height and opens the room to the trees that branch out above. New closet space is handy, and a fireplace enhances the new gathering area with a warm intimacy.

Outside the kitchen, a new deck creates an outdoor living and entertainment area. A solid railing on one side provides privacy from neighboring homes, while an open railing faces the valley and vista.

Architects: Churchill-Zlatunich-Lorimer AIA.

Kitchen extension adds dining space, gives view of valley

New deck provides outdoor entertainment area

Kitchen grew out around a tree.
Windows welcome the outdoors in.
Tiles in new dining area match
those in old kitchen.

Bold addition oriented to lakefront life style

From beach cottage to year-round house

This house, which began as a beach cottage, was small and dark, and had a tight, closed-in feeling. Located on a lake close to town, it was worth remodeling for family living.

Leaving the small living room and dining room intact, the addition created a new family area off the kitchen. Relocation of the house's entry improved traffic patterns, greatly increasing the effective area of the original living room. Oriented to beach activities, the addition had to provide plenty of storage space for boating and camping gear, as well as a pottery studio, mud room, and half bath.

The new addition has two floors. Downstairs are the family room, studio, half bath, and mud room. Upstairs are a sewing room, the master bedroom, and a bathroom. Higher ceilings, as well as doors and windows opening out to the beach, provide the open, light, spacious feeling the owners wanted.

The small size and low ceilings of the original house created a problem in blending old and new. But lapping the roof of the addition over the original house to form a clerestory above the stairwell tied the two structures together esthetically. Also, windows in the addition were scaled to the original house, and the first-floor roof overhangs the deck and entry.

Architect: Carolyn D. Geise.

Addition to this beach house enhanced its livability and provided an entire new wing, including studio, mudroom, and decks.

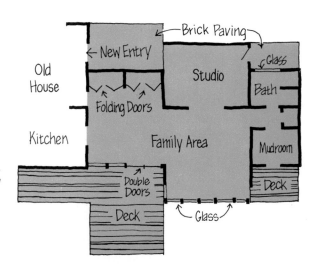

Window wall faces the beach. With its wood-shingled exterior and simple lines, house blends into its environment.

From old garage to new family room

A rainy-day retreat for the children

Sometimes you can add a room without adding more area to your house. The owners of this house did just that. They wanted more room for informal family activities and for dining off the kitchen area.

Once they decided that space for cars wasn't as important as space for people, they transformed half the garage into a new family room. There is still garage enough for a single car—as required by the local zoning ordinance.

The new room doesn't extend all the way out to the street-side wall; some former garage space was left to provide storage. Also, a new street-side window opens directly into the family room.

Separate yet easily observable from the kitchen, the new room provides an excellent retreat for the family's young children, and is a lifesaver on a rainy day. It allows the old family area adjacent to the kitchen to be used as a large informal dining area and gathering place for conversation or study.

Architects: Churchill-Zlatunich-Lorimer.

Family room has beamed ceiling, skylight, and track lighting. Low-maintenance tile floor adds informal tone.

All-purpose room does double duty

Height and light create open space for artistic family

The owners of this house wanted a large new all-purpose room with ample height and light to contrast with their otherwise dark dwelling.

They planned the 21 by 28-foot family room to be large and airy enough for all kinds of activities, from impromptu family recitals to large parties.

Supporting the 21-foot span are 4 by 16-inch beams vaulting to an 18-foot high wall—a dramatic change from the conventional 8-foot ceilings in the old house. The tall, tongue-and-groove cedar wall gives the space the owners wanted for hanging paintings. The room is large enough to accommodate a fireplace and a baby grand piano without being in the least crowded.

The room includes a freestanding closet, which serves as a room divider between entry hall and living area and provides storage space near the front door.

The new room is generously lit by ten skylights: four plastic bubbles near the short side of the room and six flat sheets of ½-inch-thick clear acrylic centered between the beams just above the tall wall.

Another attraction of the room's location is that it unites the original house with the old guest quarters, providing much-needed space for a growing family.

Architect: Leon Armatrout.

New room offers lots of storage, fireplace for coziness. Skylighted ceiling creates spacious feeling.

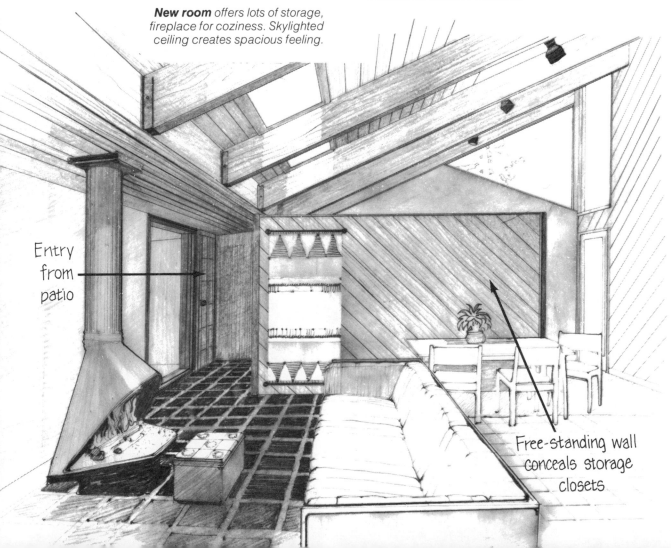

Entry from patio

Free-standing wall conceals storage closets

Sloping skylight ceiling allows light to pour into once-dark attic. Shelves provide plenty of storage, room for plants.

Kitchen skylight in same ceiling/wall as living room

From dark attic to sunny living space

Skylights brighten new living room, dining room, kitchen

Light is a major challenge in converting dark attic space into usable living space. In this house, two skylights and a small balcony accomplish the task.

Before the skylights were added, two bedrooms, a bath, and an interior stairwell filled half the attic space; the other half was used only for storage. Now the former storage area is a living room, dining room, and kitchen.

In each skylight, three 2½-foot-wide acrylic panes, carefully sealed at the edges to prevent leaks, are supported by 2-by-6 rafters. The rafters end about 2 feet above floor level, where they are joined to conventional vertical windows.

With such large areas of glass, summer heat buildup and winter heat loss are problems to reckon with. Orientation is a critical factor. These skylights face northwest; even better are north, northeast, or east exposures, which would catch less summer sun. Tinted glass can also help minimize heat accumulation, as can shades or curtains.

Architect: Elizabeth G. Burger.

Windows at end of living room open for cross ventilation

Large windows *give feeling almost like being outdoors. A small balcony extends behind large wicker chair.*

ass doors to small balcony

How to cut add-on costs

Tips for reducing expenses

Saving money is a subject dear to the hearts and wallets of all homeowners, and especially to those adding on. Whatever its size, that addition is not going to come cheap, and all suggestions for cutting costs should be warmly received.

Two cost-cutting points

First, unless you're careful, cutting costs can mean cutting quality. Don't settle for what's cheaper if it means that the finished product will suffer. Don't try to do work yourself that you're not really good at.

Second, remember that usually what you save in money you spend in time — you may spend weekend after weekend hunting sales of building materials, or you might devour great chunks of spare time cleaning up, installing insulation, or putting up gypsum wallboard.

Twelve money-saving tips

Below we've listed a number of homeowner-tested ways for saving money in adding on:

• *Do all the work yourself.* If you have time — and if you are confident that your skills as a designer and builder will create an addition that will be an asset to your property—you can save a great deal of money by doing the whole thing yourself, from start to finish. Some homeowners who have done this indicate that savings can be anywhere from 20 to 60 percent.

• *Be your own contractor.* Here again, you can spend a lot of time to save yourself money. Be prepared for hassles and hard work. (See page 13 for a more complete discussion of being your own contractor.)

• *Hire less expensive labor.* If you're going to be your own contractor, you can hire students or retired or moonlighting craftspeople and construction workers who will probably charge less than the workers a professional general contractor hires.

• *Prepare the site yourself.* Before construction begins, you can do any necessary demolition, such as tearing up concrete and pulling down walls.

• *Do all the cleanup.* Normally, a contractor will see to it that the building site is cleaned up, and will charge you for the necessary labor. You can agree with the contractor to do daily cleanup and to do all necessary cleanup and hauling after the job is completed.

• *Install the insulation.* One of the most common tasks that homeowners do during the construction process is installing insulation. It's a relatively simple job, and doing it yourself can save some labor costs.

• *Do some finishing work.* Many homeowners have saved money by doing sanding, sealing, and painting themselves. Also, you can install such hardware as cabinet handles and light fixtures.

• *Look for sales.* You can save money on materials by hunting up suppliers' distress, clearance, and carload sales.

• *Check wholesale and retail suppliers for seconds.* A second is often as good as "unflawed" and flaws are usually insignificant. Just make sure such items are structurally sound.

• *Go to the manufacturer.* Manufacturers of such materials as tile, skylights, and flooring often sell direct to the public for prices lower than retail.

• *Use less expensive grades.* With some careful shopping you can find exterior grades of wood (rough, shop, and garden grades) that will serve your purposes just as well as more costly finished lumber.

• *Use recycled house parts.* If you're ready and willing to immerse yourself completely in your room addition project, you can haunt wrecking and salvage yards (look in the Yellow Pages under "Wrecking Contractors") for treasures removed from demolished buildings. If you're after something specific, put the word in with various wreckers to keep an eye out for it. Also, watch for demolitions in progress. You can often learn in advance about the demolition of a building by reading the legal notices in a local building trade paper.

An addition that doesn't look like one

Two bedrooms, a bath, a sitting area — all faithfully Tudor

With two growing children, the owners of this house needed more space and privacy. They wanted an addition that wouldn't look like an addition but would continue the Tudor style of the existing structure.

Their two-bedroom addition above the kitchen blended perfectly with the house. Outside, the finish and trim are simply continued from old house to addition. Inside, the high beamed ceiling in the master bedroom repeats the country-manor feeling of the downstairs living room.

The master bedroom suite is large: it has a separate sitting area, a bathroom, and a small deck overlooking the back patio. In one corner is a gas-fired freestanding fireplace.

Architect: Carl Day.

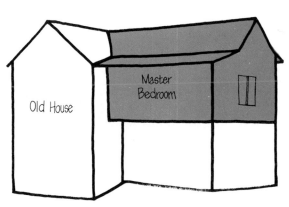

Above: New master bedroom has small sitting area, exposed beamed ceiling. *Right:* Added exterior is perfectly in keeping with Tudor styling of original house.

Small cottage grows up

Second story adds master bedroom, children's room, bath, closets

A large backyard was something the owners of this house didn't want to sacrifice. So when the small, one-story house didn't seem roomy enough for them any more, the only way to go was up.

But they didn't want just a box stuck on top; they wanted an addition that would blend in well with the existing structure, continuing its cottagelike flavor.

The new second floor adds a master bedroom, a children's bedroom, a bathroom, a walk-in closet, and a linen closet. The outside of the addition merges nicely with the exterior of the old house. Inside the new master bedroom the exposed truss ceiling is the same as that in the living room downstairs.

The new master bedroom made it possible to convert the old bedroom into a den. And to take better advantage of the backyard the owners enjoy so much, they replaced its standard door with large French doors.

Architect: James Mount.

Second-story bedroom addition overlooks front yard. Inside, spacious room has dark, exposed-truss ceiling, built-in window seat.

Even a small addition can make a big difference

Pushing out a wall creates a roomy breakfast nook

The kitchen of this house was a little too dark for its owners. Besides more light, they also wanted a breakfast area and a new deck, but they didn't want to reduce the size of their backyard.

The overhang of the kitchen's shedlike roof presented an excellent opportunity for expansion without major structural changes. The addition pushed out a kitchen wall to the limit of the roof overhang. Built inward from the new wall, an 8-foot window seat obviates the need for a full set of chairs around the table and provides a spacious feeling in very little actual available space. Vertical tongue-and-groove hemlock paneling was used for the interior.

A door and large picture window open onto a new deck, added over what was once a small concrete patio so that no backyard space was sacrificed.

Architect: Ted Granger.

Kitchen wall has pass-through to breakfast area

Window seat eliminates need for space-consuming chairs in small dining area. New nook looks into backyard. Light-colored hemlock wall paneling helps keep room bright.

Door opens to new deck

They needed a private bedroom and a room for music

They added an upstairs bedroom suite, converted a downstairs bedroom into a music room

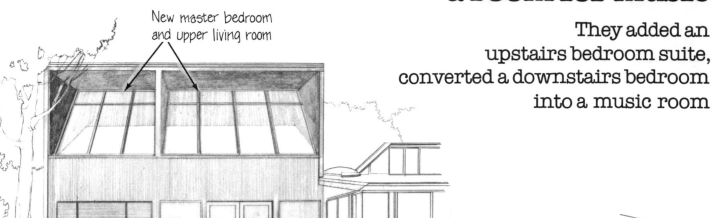

New master bedroom and upper living room

Above: Tall, slanting windows of new second story face onto patio. Below: Upper level allows intimacy with wooded surroundings.

Stairway down to front entry

Before remodeling, this house had a master bedroom right off the front doorway; it didn't provide the privacy the owners wanted. Besides, one of the owners is a piano teacher who needed a room for lessons—a room situated so as not to disrupt life in the rest of the house.

Both problems were solved by the addition of a second-floor master bedroom suite, freeing the old master bedroom for lessons and practice.

The new second floor comprises a bedroom, bath, and large walk-in closets. The living room roof was also raised to match the height of the added second floor roof line, almost doubling the room's height and creating a very striking visual effect. Large slanted windows allow light to enter and afford fine views of the surrounding wooded hillsides.

An opening in the new bedroom's wall overlooks the living room, creating an interesting balconylike effect. The opening can be closed with cupboard-type doors.

Architect: Carl Day.

Balcony bridge overlooks expanded living room. High bookshelves, plants, and art brighten upper walls. Deck also adjoins master bath.

Stairway down to front entry

Bridge to bath, bedroom overlooks living room

Upstairs addition is youngsters' domain

Large bedroom and bath harmonize with original house

You'd never know that this upstairs addition wasn't part of the original house. It was built above the lowest part of the existing structure, a center section that connected two wings.

The addition provides one large room and a bath for two young children. Right now the room can be separated into two smaller ones by an accordion-folding wooden partition. When the children are older a permanent wall may be added, creating two distinct rooms. Each end of the big room has a large window, its own built-in cabinet and closet, and hallway access to the bathroom.

The exposed beams are the actual roof supports; they're painted blue green against a light green plasterboard ceiling.

It's hard to tell old from new in this second-story addition. New siding blends well with old house.

New children's room and bath

Owners gain work/ entertainment room

Upstairs storage space becomes new loft

The architect who owns this house wanted new space for his expanding family. His design took advantage of a small attic and the attractive but inefficient cathedral ceiling in the living room.

Cutting through the roof, he fitted in a loft that extends over part of the living room. He used garage space and a closet to accommodate a stairway and landing behind an existing living room wall.

The new loft is a combination work, entertainment, and retreat space. It stays warm enough on many winter evenings that the owners can turn off the heat downstairs and read or watch television in their new perch. In summer months, the three new clerestory windows let out heat, increase air circulation, and flood the once-dark living room with light.

Architect: Russell Barto.

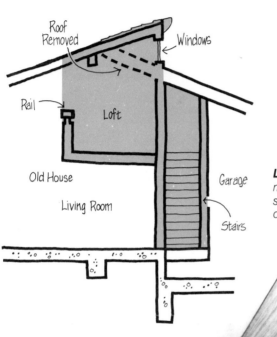

Loft was fitted into house with minimal exterior change. Inside, loft is small but well designed. Large windows improve air circulation.

Imagination transforms subdivision house

Innovative truss system supports new second floor

Both the owners of this house are artists who work at home. They wanted more room to "retreat" from their work environment—to keep living space and working space separate.

They wanted a truly unusual design for an addition to their typical, flat-roofed tract house. They got a new second floor that includes a master bedroom, vanity, bathroom, walk-in closet, small sitting room, and deck. The design gave the owners the room they wanted and satisfied their demand for something unique: the new second story rests not on top of the first, but 18 inches above it, on its own foundation. A circular stairway joins the two floors.

The structural system of the addition, known as a truss, was chosen for its capability to span long distances. In this case, it spans over the existing house. Two identical trusses, supported on each end by a pair of 12-inch-diameter wooden poles, comprise the basic structure. Besides supporting the new upper floor, the structure creates a striking visual effect.

Architect: Roger East.

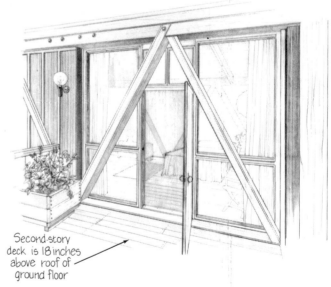

Second-story deck is 18 inches above roof of ground floor

External truss structure is repeated decoratively inside on wall of new master bedroom.

Above: *Creative notions transform a once plain tract house.* **Left:** *Decorative horse accents imaginative circular stairway.* **Below:** *Detail of truss and pole structure.*

Add-on Ideas **55**

Addition goes up for bedroom, bath

Addition goes out for kitchen, dining room

Symmetrical, *rather ordinary look of old house was changed significantly by upper-story addition. Windows face toward garden, away from neighbors.*

Lakefront cottage grows up and out

Without crowding lot, owners gain new kitchen, dining room, master bedroom

This small home on a long, narrow lakefront lot presented its owners with a number of challenges. They needed more house, and they wanted landscaping that would give privacy and at the same time make their small garden as large as possible.

The final plans called for pushing up through the roof to add a master bedroom and bath, and pushing out toward one side fence to accommodate a new kitchen and dining room. The old kitchen became a study.

With window expanses only on the garden side, and with a sweeping shed roof, the house has privacy from neighbors and excellent views channeled down the long lot toward the lake.

A street-side fence and plantings along the property's perimeter also help ensure privacy. The garden, mostly of evergreen shrubs but including deciduous trees to let in winter sunlight, creates the illusion of a much larger area.

Architect: Reid Morgan.

Jalousie windows bring fresh air into kitchen

Above: New kitchen has exposed-beam ceiling with skylight. **Left:** Odd-shaped windows in roomy bedroom have special slat blinds.

Ceiling panel lines give visual spaciousness to bedroom

Small, simple addition wrought startling changes. Glass-paneled wall gives great view of lake.

Old house is strikingly modernized by addition

Dining and lounging area flood the house with light

Before remodeling, this was a dated, dark house on a beautiful piece of lakeside land. Besides needing more space for entertaining, the owners wanted to open the house to light and to a view of the lake.

The project restructured existing interior spaces and added on a greenhouse-section dining room that helps flood the house with light and gives superb views of the lake and surrounding country-side.

The actual added space is less than 200 square feet. The old living room wall was done away with, and a new 8-foot extension was enclosed with a glass wall and slanted glass sky windows. The new space is for dining or lounging and for enjoying views of the lake and a terraced garden.

The house's existing interior was redesigned so all living areas open up and focus, through the addition, on the spectacular view of the lake.

Architects: Boutwell, Gordon, Beard and Grimes.

Slanted sky window and glass walls give lake view

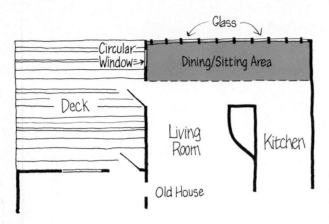

Glass

Circular Window →

Dining/Sitting Area

Deck

Living Room

Kitchen

Old House

Glassed-in addition is focus of re-designed interior space. **Below:** Circular window on end wall looks out onto large deck.

Sun deck converts into children's playroom

Spiral staircase routes traffic around main part of house

The owners of this house wanted a separate play area and workroom for their children. Like so many older homes, this one fills nearly as much of its lot as zoning allows. Some building space was available toward the back of the lot, but a playroom added at the back of the house would make access from the childrens' bedrooms awkward and block the main access from house to garden, which is through the dining room to a floor-level porch.

The solution was to convert a second-story sun deck into the playroom and connect it with a spiral staircase to the garden and outdoor play area below. The children enter their domain from their upstairs bedroom; they can pursue their activities well away from the main living areas. From the kitchen below, their parents can easily hear them and can watch their comings and goings on the outdoor stairs.

Architect: Sanford Pollack.

__New playroom__ has lots of windows, ample storage. Outdoor stairway allows comings and goings without disturbing other parts of house.

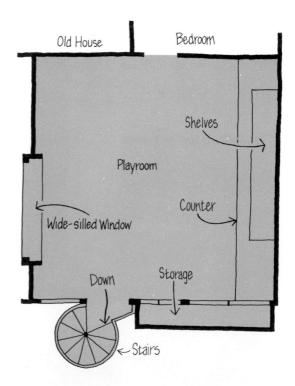

A separate addition on stilts creates a covered patio

Privacy for parents and music-minded teen-age children

The two teen-age boys who live here with their parents are, among other things, enthusiastic musicians. Their parents wanted an addition that provided more privacy for the boys — and some insulation from the sounds of their playing.

Their addition consists of two bedrooms for the boys behind the central structure of the main house, far enough away from it to be private. The boys may enter their new quarters from the main house or from a private entry off a brick courtyard. Redwood both inside and out, the new addition is a second-floor structure built on stilts. The area underneath has become a covered patio. The high, narrow windows in the young musicians' bedrooms favor a feeling of privacy while still letting in plenty of light and views of nearby large pine trees.

When the boys grow up, the addition will be used as a sewing area and guest quarters.

Architect: Daniel Solomon.

Right: Bedroom addition is mounted on stilts; covered patio underneath. **Below:** High-level bedroom windows give light, privacy.

Clerestory windows give good light

Hillside home reaches down for room

"Daylight basement" becomes bright guest room and study

If you want to expand your house without adding on, one direction to look is down. Basements are fairly common in older houses, particularly in the East and Midwest. And hillside homes often have "daylight basements" — rooms with one side above ground and both ends partially exposed.

Here is the bold renovation of a house built in the early 1900s with a shallow basement and an open-air porch under the main floor.

By opening the basement to the porch and enclosing them as a single wide-open area, what had been storage space became a combination guest room and study with a generous view out to the garden. The absence of stairwells adds to the open feeling.

The old porch floor was replaced with brick laid in sand on the ground to drain excess water from plants. The hardwood floor of the main room, a foot higher, was laid over existing concrete.

The unusual shape of the two openings to the garden (one is a door, the other a window) follows the line of the house supports; fixed glass around the window and door allows maximum light to enter the room.

Architect: A. O. Bumgardner.

Imaginatively shaped entry helps draw the outdoors into this remodeled basement.

Pair of interesting shapes cuts stylish design in basement wall.

Glass-door garden entry to basement rooms

Open stairway *descends into new living area with its hardwood floor. Entry floor, foreground, is brick.*

Conserving energy is crucial

How to let the sun work for you

When thinking about adding on, take time to reexamine your home's energy needs and deficiencies. Heating costs continue to rise, and many homeowners are finding that solar heating is an environmentally sound, economically feasible energy saving scheme.

Energy conservation comes first

Perhaps the simplest way of making the sun work for you is to design an addition that can be heated directly by the sun's radiation. (This is referred to as "passive" solar heating.) In considering such a system, ask yourself the following questions:

- What location will give the addition the greatest solar exposure?
- What are the best ways of letting in the sun?
- How can you prevent heat from escaping?
- How can you keep the addition from overheating?

To make the most of the sun's radiation, design your addition to face due south (the direction of greatest solar exposure) and use windows generously. The greater the window area in the south wall, the more heat the addition will receive. However, if you live in an area where summer heat is more of a problem than winter cold, you may want to orient the addition to the north or east to block out some of the sun's rays.

After encouraging the proper build-up of solar heat in your addition, take steps to hold it there. Heat travels from warmer to cooler areas, and if outside air is cooler than inside, heat will travel out. Examine areas where heat might escape. Uninsulated walls, roofs, and floors may usurp two-thirds of your hard-won heat through conduction, radiation, and convection. Glass and windows, as well as cracks, joints, and ill-fitting door frames may cause further loss. Solve this problem by using insulation, weatherstripping, caulking, and double-glazing.

Insulation decreases energy loss between heated and unheated spaces. When you add on, it's a simple matter to insulate exterior walls, but insulation may also be needed in the ceiling or under the floor.

After insulating, seal small cracks around doors and windows with weatherstripping. For a final "tightening up," caulk small wall cracks or joints.

From the standpoint of energy conservation, perhaps the most effective windows are those that have two or three layers of glass with dead air space between layers. But even double or triple-glazed windows may need to be covered with movable insulation panels at night to prevent heat loss.

Too much heat can be as discomforting as not enough. If overheating becomes a problem, use exterior shades or screens to help block or filter direct sunlight. Roof overhangs, trellises, and deciduous trees are also effective since they prevent the sun from reaching and overheating walls and windows.

Active energy alternatives

If your addition is a major one — such as an entire second story—you may wish to consider installing an active solar energy system to heat the entire house. Such systems involve collector panels on the roof, and pumps or fans, pipes or ducts, and tanks or rock bins in the basement. Because installing an active system is a major commitment in both cost and time, it's advisable to consult a reputable solar architect or designer.

If adding on involves a general home remodeling, you may wish to consider another heating alternative — the electric heat pump.

Here, too, installation is a major and complex task. Cooling as well as heating, heat pumps work well in temperate to hot climates, but where winter temperatures fall below 35° F., you'll probably need a back-up system.

For further energy-saving ideas, see *Sunset Homeowner's Guide to Solar Heating* and *Sunset's Insulation & Weatherstripping*.

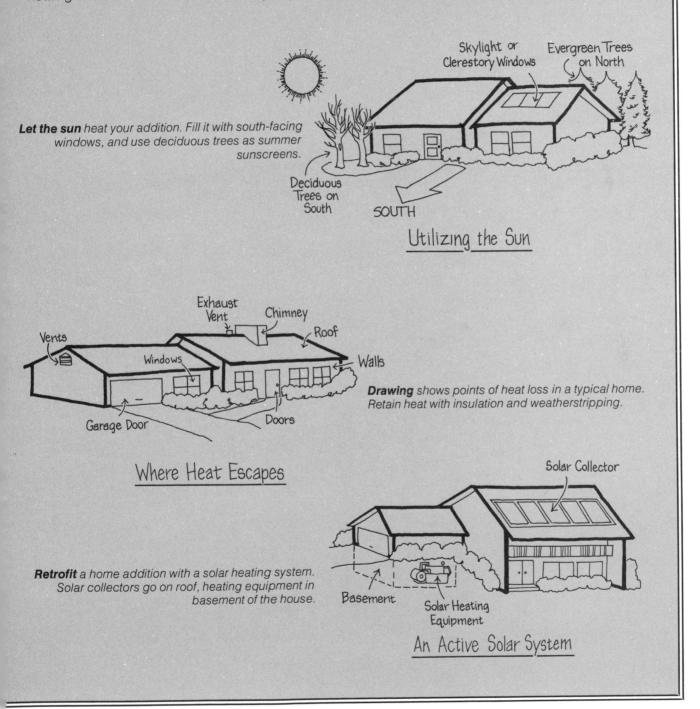

Skylight or Clerestory Windows

Evergreen Trees on North

Let the sun heat your addition. Fill it with south-facing windows, and use deciduous trees as summer sunscreens.

Deciduous Trees on South

SOUTH

Utilizing the Sun

Exhaust Vent

Chimney

Roof

Vents

Windows

Walls

Drawing shows points of heat loss in a typical home. Retain heat with insulation and weatherstripping.

Garage Door

Doors

Where Heat Escapes

Solar Collector

Retrofit a home addition with a solar heating system. Solar collectors go on roof, heating equipment in basement of the house.

Basement

Solar Heating Equipment

An Active Solar System

New family room off kitchen creates intimate relationship with outdoors

Modern sky windows blend with 1906 house

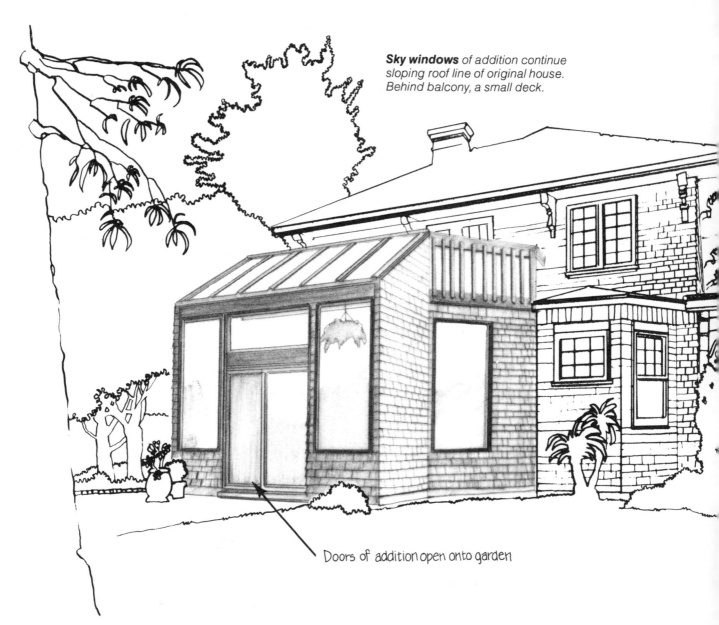

Sky windows *of addition continue sloping roof line of original house. Behind balcony, a small deck.*

Doors of addition open onto garden

The owners of this hilltop house wanted a family room with an easy, natural relationship to the outdoors and a better view of the ocean in the distance.

The lines of the 1906 house weren't marred in the slightest by the addition of a sun-filled family room at the rear. Done at the same time as a kitchen remodel, the new room blends well with the rest of the house without trying to conceal the fact that it's an addition.

The room was designed with a sloping sky window, pitched at the same angle as the roof, so the lines of the addition flow into those of the house. A small deck added behind the sky window opens an upstairs bedroom to the outdoors (a door was fitted into an old window opening).

The north-facing room is a great place for plants. Large containers rest on the brick floor; hanging ones are suspended on pulleys. Because it's a few steps down from the kitchen, the room has the benefit of an 11-foot-high ceiling. The sky window rises for 15 feet at the top.

Architect: Val Thomas.

__Brick-floored__ room is showcase for hanging plants, art works. Floodlights recessed in ceiling enhance natural lighting.

See-over kitchen half-wall

They wanted a second story and their own space

Above all, the new master bedroom is private

Originally the owners of this house converted the garage into a master bedroom, connecting it to the main house with a lanailike covered patio. After a while they began to wish for more privacy than their ground-floor addition offered them, so they decided on a second-story addition.

Like the earlier addition, the new second story blends in nicely with the original structure. It includes a master bedroom, an adjoining bathroom, a vanity with a double sink, and a large walk-in closet. Also added was a small deck overlooking the backyard, reached through sliding glass doors from either the bedroom or the bath.

Downstairs, the addition of a fireplace to the old master bedroom converted it into a family room. The floor of the enclosed patio was built up to the level of the adjoining living room and retiled. The existing patio wall was pushed out slightly, and sliding glass doors were added to open to the outdoor patio and garden. These modifications let in light and allowed the new space between the dining room and family room to become not only a circulation area for the new stairway to the second floor, but also a small gallery and music area. The glass wall and doors on the first floor reiterate those of the upstairs bedroom suite, thereby integrating the second-story addition with the main house.

Architects: Churchill-Zlatunich-Lorimer.

Both new master bedroom and bathroom open onto deck. Bathroom has large storage area.

Viewed from front, second-floor addition appears small, simple, unobtrusive.

Roomy sleeping quarters grow over a garage

Addition linked to main house by new family room

Among the most obvious places to add on is above an attached garage. The owners of this house wanted new bedrooms for their children, a good healthy distance away from the master bedroom. They didn't want to sacrifice any backyard space, so they added on above the garage.

It's frequently not possible to conceal the fact that an above-garage structure is an addition. Here the effort was not to hide anything but to create a fine-looking structure that complements the rest of the house. The roof pitch of the addition is the same as that of the main house, creating a pleasant harmony.

Besides the new bedrooms, the house gained a new family room through conversion of the service area between kitchen and garage. And the dining room was enlarged by pushing its front wall forward.

Architects: Hunter and Appel.

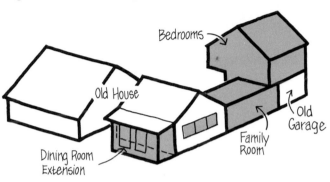

Family gained new bedrooms over the garage and converted service area into the family room shown at right.

The open, roomy feeling of this townhouse belies its small size: only 960 square feet of floor space. The effect was achieved by an upward and outward expansion that involved several steps.

First, a cross-shaped upper level was added, providing sleeping space, a study alcove, and a bridge to an outside deck while leaving large openings for light to fall through upper windows and skylights to the main floor below.

The building code required either plywood interior shear walls or a steel frame to strengthen the added height. The frame was less expensive and far more desirable, enabling the owner to do away with cloistering interior walls altogether. The only enclosures are a bathroom and a child's room at the rear of the house.

The strengthening frames consist of two tall steel rectangles, inserted through the house levels at front and rear and ballasted by concrete under the garage floor. The frames also help support the new upper floor.

Finally, a 3-foot lateral extension—just enough for support posts to clear the existing outside stairway—made room for inside stairs to the new level, ample bedroom storage on that level, and a fireplace alcove underneath.

Architect: Daniel Solomon.

Above: High windows and skylights flood stairs with light. Right: Steel frame accents living room, dining room decor.

Small San Francisco house opens up and grows

Steel frame allows expansive interiors, new bedroom loft

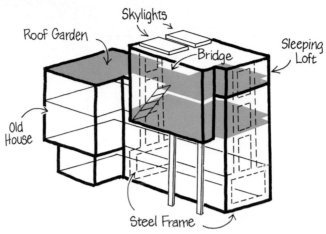

Roof Garden

Skylights

Bridge

Sleeping Loft

Old House

Steel Frame

Above: Steel frames and lateral extension make room for addition. *Left:* Loft bedroom faces bridge leading to roof garden.

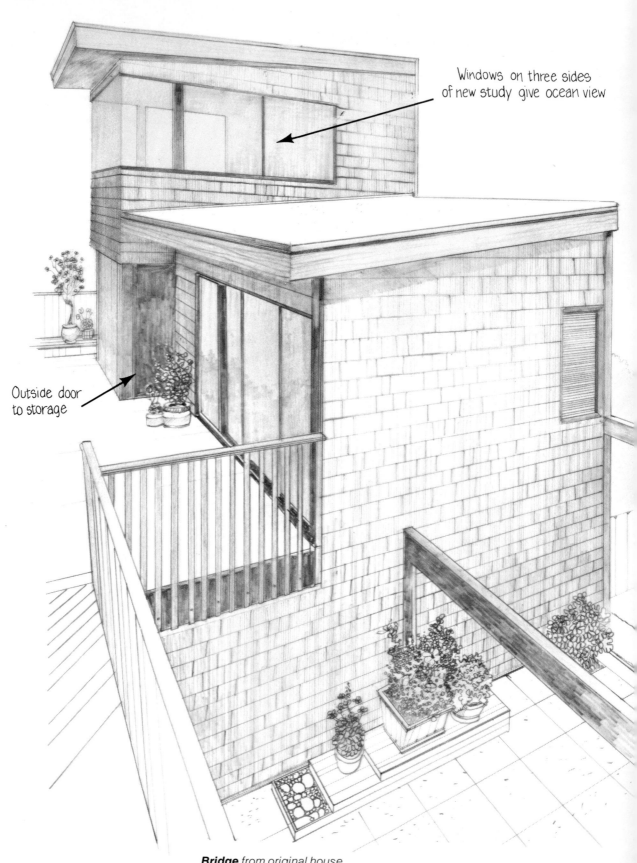

Windows on three sides
of new study give ocean view

Outside door
to storage

Bridge *from original house
leads to new playroom / guest
area and second-story study.*

No more room in the house, so they added on top of garage

Two-tiered expansion provides "crow's nest" study plus children's play area

Situated on a tiny lot, this house filled all available ground space. As their family grew, the owners needed more room for two active children and a study where the adults could enjoy quiet and privacy.

The only way to go was up, and the only place to go up was over the garage. The outcome was a two-room, two-level addition. The lower room accommodates guests when they are present, serving as a children's playroom at other times. Up a steep stairway is a "crow's nest" study, high enough to give a fine ocean view, and effectively separated from the play area.

Overlooking a back patio, a red tiled deck and bridge connect the new rooms with the main house. Exterior cedar shingles match the house siding.

Architect: John Blanton.

Stair ladder *connects the playroom/guest room with hideaway study located above it.*

Stair ladder goes from playroom to "crow's nest" study

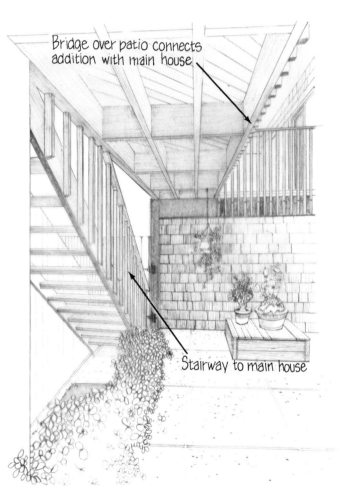

Bridge over patio connects addition with main house

Stairway to main house

Underneath *the new deck/bridge is a cement patio. Stairway at left leads up to main house.*

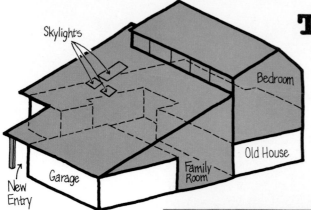

Skylights

Bedroom

Old House

Family Room

Garage

New Entry

Dotted lines show original house.

Above: Once-flat house doubles in size, gains second story. *Right:* High ceiling, windows, doors open up kitchen to new family room.

They wanted more space and visual appeal

They got six rooms and a brand new look

Originally this house was an ordinary-looking flat-roofed structure. The owners needed a great deal more space, and they wanted to improve the appearance of their home.

Their sloping-roofed addition nearly doubled the size of the house and transformed a plain exterior into a far more interesting one.

Inside are a new family room, three new bedrooms, and two new bathrooms. The new family room, built where a central atrium used to be, is now the heart of the house. It's a full two stories (18 feet) high. Bronzed glass in the room's large windows keeps down glare while preserving a light, open feeling.

All exterior walls were covered with stucco. The addition and the original house merge perfectly, presenting a far more attractive façade to the world than did the old house.

Architect: William Gratiot.

Above: Sloping roof, stucco exterior unite old and new. **Left:** New master bedroom overlooks backyard.

Once a cramped attic, now a comfortable studio/guest room

Lounge-niches accommodate overnight guests

Fabric-covered, 5-inch foam pad for sitting, sleeping

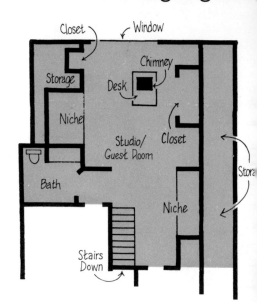

Closet
Window
Storage
Chimney
Desk
Niche
Closet
Studio/ Guest Room
Storage
Bath
Niche
Stairs Down

__Niches__ for sitting and sleeping are built under sloping portion of roof. Above them, skylights let in daylight, night sky views.

Sloping skylights give view of night sky

Once a cramped space under a sloping roof, this second-floor conversion is like getting an addition without adding any extra space. It has become a studio/guest room as airy and open as a tree house.

What opened things up was a full glass gable end wall overlooking the garden. Removing the dropped ceiling and adding new beams made a big difference, as did the two new sleeping or lounging niches.

The niches leave a maximum of floor space open and free of furniture in a narrow room where standing space under the roof slope measures only 12 feet across. The skylights above each niche help balance the light from the glass gable at the room's end; without them the room would resemble a tunnel.

To save more space, a work table surrounds the furnace chimney that ascends through the middle of the room. The chimney itself is sheathed in wood strips of varying thickness — a timbered version of flagstones.

Designer: Richard W. Painter.

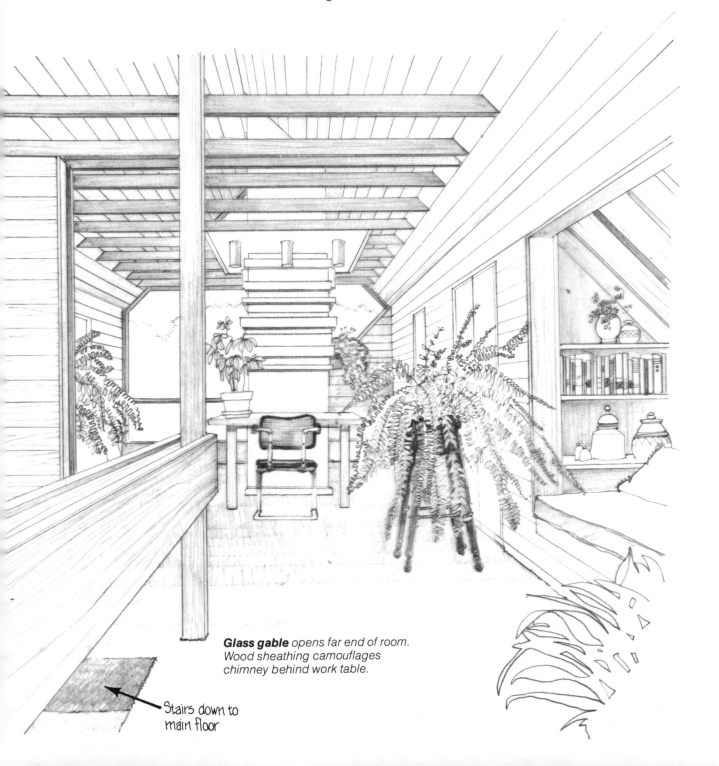

Glass gable opens far end of room. Wood sheathing camouflages chimney behind work table.

Stairs down to main floor

The attic idea

Gaining low-cost, usable space

Compared with building an addition, converting an existing attic can be a relatively low-cost way to gain usable space and increase the value of your home. Sometimes thought of as dark, cramped spaces, attics can be transformed into intriguing living areas, ranging from quiet adult retreats to children's playrooms.

Though an attic conversion may be as simple as painting a wall or carpeting a floor, more intricate conversions, such as adding a master bedroom suite, require detailed planning and expert consultation.

Electricity, heating, plumbing

Before you start, ask yourself these questions: Will converting the attic require any major structural changes? Are electrical, heating, and plumbing lines near the attic, or will they have to be installed? If the attic is dark, how can it be opened to light? Will the floor need greater support when the attic is used as a living space?

Some attics are built with expansion in mind, so electrical, heating, and plumbing lines may be nearby. If this is not the case in your attic, it's wise to consult a professional, since increasing a house's electrical capacity may involve installing whole new circuits. Installing heating may require bringing ducts up from the basement. But some furnaces cannot handle an extra load, and you may have to install electric heat in the new space. Adding plumbing usually means breaking into drain pipes and adding new vents. If you're putting in a bathroom, you can simplify plumbing matters by trying to locate it over an existing one on the floor below, though not at the cost of total design.

Insulation and lighting

An attic room will probably need insulation. In most cases, existing insulation will be spread or stapled between the ceiling joists (those on which your new floor will rest). Leave it there for sound deadening and install new insulation on attic ceilings and in walls.

If your attic is dark, install gable or shed dormer windows to add light as well as headroom. Or use sloping skylights to bring in light and add drama. You can even cut out a section of roof and install a balcony with sliding glass doors. Since warm air rises, attics are often summertime hot spots, so plan windows and doors to give good cross ventilation.

Collar support beams may reduce attic space; they can usually be replaced with small plywood sections (gussets) that will support rafters while giving more headroom. To reinforce attic floors, double the joists. Insulation plus carpeting will help prevent noise from reaching the rest of the house.

Track lights *illuminate attic conversation area. Drawers provide storage.*

Attic gable *makes perfect children's study area. Toys stored on shelves.*

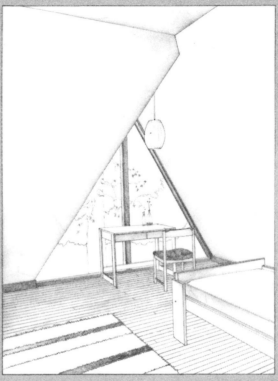

Triangular *floor-to-ceiling window opens up attic to view of trees.*

Skylights *brighten this stairway leading from second floor to attic.*

Skylight *brings airy feeling into small attic loft bedroom.*

Cramped living quarters? One way to go is up

Two-level addition combines studio, family room, bathroom, storage

With two teen-age boys and one artist parent, the family who lives in this house needed more space for activities and separate teen-age gatherings, and a well-lighted studio for painting.

The answer is a two-story addition off one end of the house. It combines a studio with superb natural lighting, a new family activity room, some storage space, and a bathroom.

Access to the new rooms is through the dining room, which gained 4 feet in width as a result of the remodeling project.

A curved staircase joins the two floors of the added structure.

Architects: Allan-Scarbro Associates.

Window wall of second-story studio lets in natural light and tree view.

New art studio has plenty of counter space for spreading out materials, small sink for cleaning up.